Making Good in Management

Making Good in Management

Reflections on the Challenges and Opportunities of a Business Career

CLARENCE B. RANDALL

Retired Chairman of the Board
Inland Steel Company

McGRAW-HILL BOOK COMPANY

New York   Toronto   London

MAKING GOOD IN MANAGEMENT

Contents

CHAPTER 1. *The Big Decision* 5

CHAPTER 2. *Big Business or Small Business?* 21

CHAPTER 3. *What Education?* 37

CHAPTER 4. *What Adjustments?* 53

CHAPTER 5. *What Is Business?* 69

CHAPTER 6. *What Are the Rewards?* 85

CHAPTER 7. *What Are the Ethical Problems?* 101

CHAPTER 8. *What Is Leadership?* 117

CHAPTER 9. *What Are the Obligations?* 133

CHAPTER 10. *What Lies Ahead?* 149

Contents

Introduction

The businessman who like myself has reached that exciting period of euphoria known as retirement will, if he is wise, persistently seek out the companionship of younger men. And if I may venture the suggestion, those who occupy the junior echelon of management, or who are approaching it for the first time, will likewise find it rewarding to explore their problems with those who are many years their senior. This is not always easy to achieve, since obvious limitations, both physical and psychological, tend to separate the two groups, but these barriers must be broken down. The backward look and the forward look are both important in the development of our society, and the improvement of management, in my opinion, requires a continuous dialogue between the voice of experience and the voice of youth.

The publishers of this little volume seem to hold this opinion too, so when they asked me to put on

1

paper some of my reflections upon the problems of management, I leaped at the opportunity with high enthusiasm, addressing myself directly to younger men in exactly the same manner that I would if a group of them were sitting around a luncheon table with me exchanging viewpoints. Business has been both my livelihood and my passion, and I have tried to review not only the opportunities and the rewards that are to be found in a business career, as I see them, but the responsibilities as well.

Based upon my own experience, the principal word of caution which I should like to urge upon young men is that they should not overplan their lives too far in advance. It is the unexpected that tests a man's caliber. He must be ready at all times to move off in a new direction if a suddenly unforeseeable circumstance shoves him that way. To change the metaphor, let him remember that sooner or later the ball gets thrown to each one of us at least once. The thing to do is not to stand around worrying because the pass has not been thrown, but rather to concentrate on being ready to run with the ball when it does come.

This means that the man must do the immediate task that is before him better than it has ever been done before, no matter how humble or unimportant it may seem at the time, and he must carry it through without frequent glances over his shoulder to see if anyone is watching. Advancement is just that simple, and only two things are required. The man must know his job, and he must know himself. Believing confidently in his own capacity to master this particular assignment, he must bring to it each day the maximum effort of which he is capable, and so overflow it with effectiveness that others must of necessity recognize his ability.

There is a special hazard in all this, however—one which I have tried to outline in this book. The individual must not become so determined to get ahead that he thinks only of himself. This can become the Achilles' heel of a society such as ours, which is based upon the concept of private enterprise, and it is the point at which both socialism and communism direct their most telling blows.

Duty to one's country must always come first. Transcending the significance of being a good management man is that of being a good citizen. Effort on behalf of the community as a whole must come ahead of effort for one's self. I must say this, however, on behalf of the young men of today as I know them: they understand this better than my generation did.

One final word. I have seen many of the other great professions and vocations at first hand, and I can imagine no career that offers more in the deep human satisfactions that make life worthwhile than one in business management.

1

The Big Decision

*Two words that distinguish
the older generation of executives from
their successors are "chance" as against
"choice." For many of today's executives
"happened" into business, whereas,
for tomorrow's industrial leaders,
business as a career will increasingly
have been a conscious choice. And many
of their numbers, in consequence,
will be not the instruments—
but the architects—of change.*

When spring comes to the campus of an American college, one thought is uppermost in the minds of the seniors. You will see them huddled on street corners talking it over, and you know that in the fraternity houses and dormitories it is the chief topic of conversation.

Those who have not as yet done so are trying to decide what career to choose when they graduate, and they are desperately anxious to be right. Life has caught up to them.

Shall it be law? Or shall it be medicine, teaching, scientific research, the ministry, the government service, or what? Or shall they just get a job in the old-fashioned way, and thus go into business?

To many, I am afraid, the latter prospect seems pretty dull, a sort of last chance for making a living, and sometimes not to be undertaken at all if a more glamorous calling can be found.

I have never seen any statistics on the subject, but I suspect that the young men who go into engineering, science, and medicine are the first to make their decisions, and that those who enter business are apt to be the last. Medicine, of necessity, is decided upon early, for there are pre-med courses to be taken as an undergraduate, and if that bridge is not crossed there is no possibility of going ahead. Often this choice is an instinctive throwback to a childhood accident or illness, and to the admiration for the physician or surgeon who was called in by the family. In the same way a geologist is sometimes born when a boy starts collecting brightly colored stones. But this is not generally true of business. I am quite sure, for example, that I did not come into the steel industry because my father ran the general store in the lovely little country town of Newark Valley, New York.

No, let's face it. Most men who today hold positions of responsibility in the business community arrived there without conscious choice. Life shoved them at various times in their careers, and they responded to the push. In one case the father and head of the family may have died early, requiring the eldest son to leave school, get a job, and support his mother. He just took the first job he could get, and learned to like it. Another may have suddenly gone off to war, married in uniform, and after his discharge found that he had to get on a payroll fast in order to support his bride. Still another may have started by practicing law, as I did, and was persuaded later, as I, to close his law books forever and assume administrative responsibilities.

I often think of this as I find myself in the presence of a large audience of businessmen. As I look out at all their faces, I wonder by what varied and diverse paths they arrived at their present stations in life. One thing is certain. It was seldom by conscious choice or advance planning. They started where they did because they had to, and then, exercising their own initiative, compelled life to open out for them.

This is America. Reflected in this process of natural selection for business leadership is the strength and stamina of our national character. When each man faces squarely up to the task ahead of him, whether or not he chose it voluntarily, and makes it a matter of personal pride to give it the very best effort that his talent permits, we measure up as a nation.

I hope that this use of our wide-open door of opportunity as a way of meeting personal and family crises may always be a part of our pattern of society, but at the same time I would like to see the hit or miss recruitment of business personnel based on such per-

sonal emergencies cut down to an irreducible mini-
mum. I want to see seniors in college choose business
as a career with the same eager decisiveness with
which their classmates select law, or medicine, or science, and I want to see them behave this way because
they know precisely what they are doing. I want to see
them plunge into business with high enthusiasm, instead of just drifting into it because they can think of
nothing else to do.

In Great Britain the business community has had
this kind of problem for some time. The "public
schools" like Eton (perversely so called in spite of the
fact that they are private and difficult to get into)
send their best graduates to Oxford and Cambridge,
and these two universities in turn give their best graduates to the public service. After the Establishment
(government) has taken its pick, the next careers in
order of preference are the professions. Those who are
left go into business.

I do not mean to suggest that a career in business
has intrinsically anything about it which entitles it to
any priority in the selection of its proper quota of
brains and character, but I do think that it is high
time that those of us who believe in the great human
values to be found in a business career should bring
it to pass that more young people, both men and
women, select it with their eyes open, and because

they choose to. We want them to stretch out their hands toward it as the ladder to achievement, and not seek it as an escape hatch to lead them out of frustration. We want to compete on even terms for the best that our youth has to offer.

To do this we must somehow convey to those who are at the decision point in their lives the full scope of the rewards and satisfactions that a career in business has to offer, and we must give them also a vivid picture of the continuing stimulus and excitement that surround it. At the present time we are not selling our product, and this is because management as a group is singularly inarticulate about itself.

To begin with the word "business" is an all-embracing term. It is not one calling but a multitude of callings, including such diverse pursuits as advertising, banking, public accounting, mining, and the production of baby foods, automobiles, jewelry, and steel. Each such subdivision of the world of industry and commerce should have a gifted spokesman, one both knowledgeable and proud of his vocation, who can give to young men and women, via both the spoken and the written word, a complete description of what opportunities his business has to offer, and what talents it requires for success.

The same element of variety prevails among the various departments of any particular business.

Some men find the outlet for their abilities in production, some in merchandising, some in research,
some in human relations, some in fiscal policy, and
so on through the entire gamut of business activity.
No two businesses are alike, no two jobs. But for
every man there is the right place, if he will only seek
it intelligently and persistently, one in which he may
grow, and one in which he may know, deep in his
heart, that he is pulling his weight.

How can the senior in college, however, know
either enough about himself, or about business, to
find that right spot? His friend who is considering the
practice of law goes into a courtroom and listens to
the arguments, and the one who thinks he will choose
surgery goes to a hospital to observe operations, but
there is no corresponding opportunity available to
the young man who wants to find a career in management. There are, however, many things he can do
that will approximate it.

Let him first of all select a dozen different possible
kinds of employment, and then go and talk with older
men who have given years of their lives to such work.
Perhaps his father can arrange these calls, or one of
the professors at his college, or better still, let him
just select in each case a man whose name is known
to him, and write him cold, asking for an interview.
Almost invariably he will be kindly received. We sen-

iors love to talk with younger men, and we are complimented to be asked. Furthermore, we are hard to stop when we start talking about our jobs. The chances are good, too, that from such a call there will develop a later invitation to visit the plant, store, or mine with which the man is associated. There is even the long chance that a job itself will materialize through this relationship. Somehow there is a special added attraction for the beginner in a job that he finds on his own.

Summer employment is also a very desirable testing ground for the man who is approaching the decision time in his life. After all, the best way to learn whether you want to work at a particular job is to try it, and this can be done during vacation time, with no obligation attached whatever. There is nothing more helpful in making up one's mind than to hear the whistle, smell the smoke, hear the assorted noises, and sense the general attitude of those involved in the processes going on about you. Many, of course, have to earn money in the summer in order to continue their education at all, and so obtain their firsthand knowledge of business as a by-product. But where the financial situation is a bit easier, vacation work seems to be going out of fashion. I am not sure that this is right. The father who had to work during his own college vacations is apt to want to spare his son, and the son is either trying out for an athletic team, or planning a trip, possibly even to Europe, feeling that he must do these things while he can before the curtain comes down. This produces the paradox that the boy from a family with means is not as well prepared to make a decision about business as a career as the boy whose family has little.

Trial and error can, of course, be continued after the student has graduated from college and taken his first job. He should not be hesitant to change employment, or employer, or both, during his early years at work, providing he does so thoughtfully, and for good reason. But he must not do this too often, or the record of positions formerly held which he will have to attach to the next application will suggest to his prospective new employer that he is a rolling stone. On the other hand, he must not delay too long if he is genuinely unhappy. Except for extraordinary circumstances, a man today must make his last job change before he is forty. Two monetary motives will be operating upon him at the same time—present earnings and future security—and since pension plans are designed to reduce turnover, once he is past forty it is not likely that the new employer will be able to equal for him the prospective income at retirement which he will receive if he stays where he is.

One further caution needs to be rendered to the

college senior, and this touches on ethics. He should never take a job unless at the time, in good faith, he intends to keep it. It is not fair, for example, to accept a place on the highly developed recruitment program of a large corporation merely to receive the training, while all the while he is secretly planning later to join the staff of a smaller competitor. The trainee does not earn his salt, and the corporation has been cheated unless the man gives return value through later service.

A word also needs to be said about starting pay. Young men are apt to attach altogether too much significance to this factor in choosing their life's work, particularly those who are married, or who hope to be so soon. Their minds are focused on the present, when they should be on the future. Young men should be taking the long look ahead, and should be weighing the ultimate opportunity that will be available to them, rather than thinking in terms of that first pay check. In fact, this preoccupation is one of the first things that the discerning recruiting officer looks for. He puts a black mark against the candidate whose first question is "How much?" and who shows much keener interest in immediate cash than in the big chance ahead.

Another common failing among job seekers is a tendency to be too strongly influenced by a desire to live in a particular geographical area. This again is the occupational disease of those about to be married, for whom the mental image of the little house and garden surrounded by a white picket fence and situated in a land of perpetual sunshine can become a fixation. The sober truth is that work has to be performed where the job is, and that some of the best jobs are in places that call for sacrifice. The countervailing truth, moreover, is that the happiness of family life lies within the home, and that those whose married happiness is based on the complete sharing of each experience can build an ideal home atmosphere anywhere.

Family relationships with the senior generation also have to be faced squarely. Here young men and women must stand firm. The choice of a career is the first basic decision of their lives, and they are entitled to make it absolutely on their own. They need guidance in the sense that without the benefit of their elders' experience they cannot be sure that they have fairly evaluated all the possibilities, but once they have seen all sides of the problem, they alone should decide. It is even better that they make mistakes and learn the hard way than that their powers of self reliance become atrophied.

This problem becomes acute in the case of a family business, and doubly so when the son bears his fa-

ther's name. And here it is often the young man himself who is to blame for not breaking the deadlock.
He has deep affection for his father and such respect
for all he has accomplished that he just cannot bring
himself to tell the truth, which is that he loathes the
business and would like to enter the career diplo-
matic service, for example. Courage and insight are
required to resolve such situations, but this can be
done. Happily, what sometimes ensues is that the
son does actually make a free choice to carry on the
business, and when this happens a new team is
formed between equals.

A further caution needs to be extended to one who
is considering business. He must not expect to see all
the way through to the end of his career at the time
when it is beginning. Sufficient unto the day are the
problems thereof. Let him simply choose the direction toward which he will start and trust to the future.

This is one of the chief distinctions between business and the professions. Take law, or medicine, or
teaching, for example. They make tremendous progress within each generation but the basic range of
problems remains broadly the same. In other words,
the young intern can foresee reasonably well the sort
of challenges he will face as he grows older. Not so
for the young man who merely takes a job. Change

is the very essence of business, and adaptability to change the essential quality of the successful member of a management team. The human body is the same mechanism that it was when first created, even though many of its mysteries have not yet been resolved by medical science. But business is a field which reflects, through structural and ideological changes, every new social and technological advance, and tomorrow we may be dealing with problems which today are not even known to exist.

In my own life, for example, when I was a senior in college, no professor in the United States gave a course in the subject of industrial relations, yet when I first came to the management level a major part of my time was devoted to problems arising from relationships with organized labor.

Science, engineering, fashion, war—these and many similar forces that surge suddenly from within the depths of our society transform business overnight, and offer new challenges to management. In my day I have seen whole new industries born, and I have also seen them die. Who could have foreseen either aviation or electronics, for example, when I was trying to choose a career? Yet lawyers still try cases, and surgeons still remove appendixes, in much the same manner that they did then. On the other hand, the steam engine, which was then the chief source of power, as well as the product of an important segment of heavy industry, will soon be found only in museums. Advertising was highly developed, we thought, but it was soon to be completely transformed by radio, and later by television. Consumer studies had not been attempted, nor had the computer yet replaced tall men standing at high desks for the posting of ledgers.

With each such technological change there must come an equivalent development in management techniques, and each such revolution opens out new opportunities to the individual. This is the perennial miracle of business, so far as the individual himself is concerned. An outlet for expression may suddenly be found for a hidden talent which, in his earlier years, he did not even suspect that he possessed.

So let no young man be perturbed because he cannot see the end from the beginning. Let him simply make the best start that he can, with faith in himself.

2

Big Business or Small Business?

*Big pond, small pond. . . . For those whose
temperaments and inclinations do not,
early in their careers, dictate the
choice between the large corporation and
the smaller company, there are important
considerations to weigh. For both
offer distinct, and different, advantages.*

When the seniors in their huddle on campus get around to the subject of what sort of a job to look for, someone always says, "Stay away from the big companies, or you'll get lost."

I know about that fear because I was born with it. My father kept the general store in the little village of Newark Valley, New York. In back of our house was the only industrial establishment in the town, a tannery. It was owned by one of the "trusts," as my father called the large corporations, and he was disgusted with it. The fact that it filled the neighborhood with an evil smell did not help any. Anyway, a distrust of big business was bred in me.

On the other hand, my uncle, in the neighboring village of Richford, owned and ran the local creamery to which the farmers brought their milk, and his way of life was regarded as exemplary. Not far away, in

the same village, another uncle by marriage made a
fair living by manufacturing small tools, sometimes
with a payroll that ran to as many as twelve people.
So by birth and instinct I was committed to the concept that small business was the true American way
of life. Yet when the accidents of life suddenly cata-
pulted me into big business, I found great satisfaction.

Let me therefore argue the pro and the con of
small business versus big business in terms of the
opportunity offered by each for those seeking to
launch their careers.

Take small business first.

There seems to be a false idea in the public mind
that because our country has grown so rapidly, and
because our economy has reached such enormous
proportions, there is no longer a place for the lone
entrepreneur—the man who starts from scratch as
our ancestors did, and creates a new mode of livelihood. This is not necessarily true. The service industries, for example, now equal in dollar volume those
that produce commodities, and one has only to think
of the sudden dappling of our countryside with fine
new motels along our principal highways, or of the
ubiquitous laundromat, to realize that just a few
short years ago this important service field was entered by many who possessed initiative and the will

to work, even though little capital was available. Or take electronics. Many a new corporation whose name is to be found on every list of the leaders in this burgeoning industry was born only a few years back in a garage workshop. The Commerce Department has studied this subject exhaustively, and their statistics prove conclusively that, notwithstanding the high risks involved, starting from scratch is just as common a phenomenon in this country today as it ever was.

There is no denying the fact that in an enterprise of limited size there is an atmosphere of intimacy among the members of the staff that is very congenial to the man breaking in. He soon knows everybody. He sees the boss all of the time, and the boss sees him. All problems are shared, and everybody knows everything that is going on. There is no sharp delineation of duties, and no spare personnel. Each man is supposed to know enough about what the rest are doing so that in case of emergency he can take over the desk of any other man on the team. This makes for rapid growth for the individual. For this reason it is quite possible for a young man to arrive at the decision-making level in a small enterprise at an earlier age than he would in a large company.

One can find confirmation of this in any town or city by studying a list of those who are active in civic affairs. The young man who attracts favorable attention in the community early is very often the one who comes from a small company. And for that matter, a look at the roster of men who have been president of the National Association of Manufacturers or of the United States Chamber of Commerce will reveal that seldom even at that level does the top man come from big business. There may be other reasons which contribute to this phenomenon, but it certainly proves that small business is an excellent training ground for leadership.

Now for the liability side of the balance sheet for the young man who is considering small business as a career.

First of all, the risk is greater. Small companies cannot be protected by diversification. They must concentrate on one product, or one aspect of service, and when the tornadoes of economic change sweep across our country they are the ones that are crippled first. A scientific discovery, a new invention, or even an unpredictable change in public taste may eliminate them completely from the field of competition, no matter how effective their management may be.

Secondly, the prospect for the ultimate personal security of the individual is less. The word "retirement" never enters into the conversation of the seniors huddled on campus, but in the fullness of time that consideration bulks large. How to maintain one's standard of living with salary cut off becomes suddenly and dramatically important. By and large, the smaller companies do not have the fully integrated insurance and pension plans that are found in the large corporations.

In terms of personal relationships it sometimes turns out that the boss is a very strange fellow indeed. He is almost certain to be an intense individualist. The very fact that he is there, and not in a larger unit, indicates that he is not by nature a team player. He may be a positive genius in terms of the development of a product, or of a new idea in merchandising, and still not have sensitivity in the handling of people. The company is apt to be built in his image, with little real delegation of authority, and that is not the right sort of atmosphere for the development of talent among juniors.

If it is the young man himself who decides to go off the deep end by starting his own business—and the chances of this occurring are in direct ratio to the number of years of graduate training he has taken at the university—he brings a new problem into his life, although he may not be aware of it as a problem until later years. At the start he is the sole owner, and as the business grows he is still the sole owner. The more successful he is, the prouder he becomes of his achievement, and the more jealous he is of letting anyone else share either his good fortune or his authority. As a consequence, when he reaches normal retirement age he feels that he cannot—must not— stop; and so he goes on indefinitely, to the great distress of his family and friends. By this time he is violating every rule of proper investment, for he has all his eggs in one basket. When his life finally comes to its close, he leaves his heirs with a serious problem. There is no way to meet the inheritance tax except by a sale of the entire business, and the forced liquidation which follows destroys much of the value he has built up.

There is also a special health hazard that arises from the maintaining of a highly successful small business. The individuals who are involved work much too hard. They are seldom organized in depth with respect to personnel, and they meet every emergency by putting in more hours themselves instead of adding to the staff. They think of each new surge as one that may be temporary. They plan for the future with respect to the product, but not with respect to people. They carry on no orderly recruitment or training programs, and when they do finally decide to add a man, they hire him away from a large competitor.

Furthermore, the individual is apt to be the sort who boasts, "Haven't had a vacation in five years—

been too busy." He has also been too busy to arrange a program of annual physical examinations, either for himself or for his subordinates, as would be done in a large company. Then one day as he approaches middle life he is felled by a coronary thrombosis, and the entire business is paralyzed because he has made no plan for this contingency. There is no one to take his place. The business falls apart, and the young man who had signed on so hopefully has to start over somewhere else.

So much for small business. Now for the pro and the con of the large corporation as the place of opportunity for a young man.

Just as it is not certain when a lamb becomes a sheep, so there is no ready standard by which to divide these two categories. However for purposes of this discussion the opposing types of opportunity stand out quite clearly.

Young men, with their eyes on the present more than on the future, often miss the obvious fact that the ultimate possible target for their effort simply has to be bigger in big business than it is in small business. Certainly that is where the big money is. Although the self-owned type of successful small business occasionally cheats on taxes by paying the owner-boss a salary that is out of line with the prevailing rate for such enterprises, broadly speaking, compensation in all types of business is related to the load carried. The greater the responsibility, the greater the opportunity for displaying talent, and the greater the contribution to society. Since responsibility obviously increases with size, it follows that the big salaries will be found in the large corporations.

Security for the future will also almost inevitably be greater in the nationally known companies. There will be a pension plan for which funds will systematically be set aside each year, and those reserves will be placed in a trust fund that keeps its assets invested in a diversified portfolio. Some provision may be made for the widow, in the event that the wife should survive her husband. There will also be a medical staff which may be readily consulted, a program of periodic physical check-ups, and a varied assortment of group insurance. In many cases there will also be available a psychological consultant with whom personal and family problems may be frankly talked out.

One important consideration that should be urged on behalf of employment by a large company is that promotion will be strictly on merit. As compared with practices in smaller companies, nepotism is all but nonexistent. The competitive pace is too hot, and the ownership too widely spread, to permit the business to be used for the special benefit of sons and nephews. Some corporations even go so far as to have a strict rule that no relative of a senior official may be employed under any circumstances, but even where such hiring is permitted, the young relative can expect no favors. Too many eyes are watching. In fact, the father usually leans over backward so far that his son must be not only just as good as the other fellow but much better, in order to get ahead.

The variety of experience that is available in big business should also be borne in mind. In both line and staff jobs there is infinite diversity in the range of skills and talents that are required, so that if a young man has at the start misjudged his own capacity he can make a lateral move and begin again in a capacity more suited to his gifts, thus avoiding the loss of his job. Furthermore, the spread of opportunity is so wide that as the years go along he is almost certain to encounter types of responsibility which he did not even know existed when he made his initial choice, among which may be one exactly to his taste.

Furthermore, his training and development will be more effectively stimulated and supervised in a large company than would be possible in a small organization with its staff limitations. Other contemporaries will be moving along in parallel paths with him in the early years, and he and they will share an invigorating camaraderie as they encounter new challenges, to a pace that has been carefully planned for them in advance. Then once the young man has become recognized as one who is rising through the ranks, new intellectual adventures will open to him through intracompany seminars and advanced management training courses at various universities. In other words, if he is both able and eager to improve his mind and widen his horizons while employed, the chances to do so will ordinarily be greater in big business than in small business.

Now as to the liability side of the balance sheet when comparing the large corporations with the small:

The fear of being lost in the crowd, which is so prevalent among college seniors when they are considering openings in large companies, is a natural one, and obviously one that is not altogether without foundation. No man who is ambitious, and who is inwardly confident of his own ability, wants to feel that he may become submerged in bigness and disappear in anonymity until all that remains to mark him is a number in a file. Certainly that does not happen in a small company, where by the very nature of the circumstances he is constantly under direct observation.

Yet those of us who have been privileged to occupy management positions in large companies know how false this notion is for the most part. The young man of promise who has been signed on by the recruiting officer of a large corporation, though he may be overawed by the bigness of the institution when he goes to work at his first job, is not really alone at all. He is being watched all the time, but it is being done so skillfully that he is entirely unaware of it. Even when told about it, he still finds it incredible, and he may never believe it until he becomes a part of management and does the watching himself. The fact is that brains and character are in short supply everywhere these days, and nothing in the world is more important to a big company than to search out talent and nourish it assiduously. If a young man is forgotten, then someone in the higher echelons of supervision has made a serious error. If it happens too often, the supervisor will be in trouble.

One limitation, however, must be recognized in advance and fully accepted by the college senior who accepts a job with a large company, or he will be unhappy. His progress in the early years will be slower than that of his roommate who decided to go in with a small company. He must wait for the parade to move ahead before his turn for promotion comes. This is the price which he must pay for the greater security and the larger ultimate target of responsibility and remuneration. His classmate will seem to forge ahead rapidly, both in salary and in the scope of his authority, but after a few years this will change. The friend will hit a plateau, circumscribed by the smaller size and scope of the business, and in due course he will be passed by the slower-moving man in the large company.

There is one further limitation about employment by a large corporation which must also be squarely faced and accepted in advance: the fact that it may involve changes of residence from one city to another as the individual rises in the scale of management. Here the classmate who went the other way may have the advantage, for small businesses do not have branches. The management of a large corporation must flow from one branch to another in response to need. This may mean a succession of rented homes or apartments in the earlier years, which is not too pleasant even when accompanied by generous moving allowances, but it is part of the price that must be paid for the broader opportunity and the greater ultimate security.

In discussing such questions, it is easy to fall into the habit of using the masculine pronoun and writing about young men, but I mean to draw no line between young men and young women. Nowadays senior girls also gather in their dormitories talking about jobs, and it is interesting to speculate whether they will find greater opportunity in the smaller or the larger companies. I rather suspect that here the balance lies in favor of small business, for the very reason that reserves of personnel there are limited, and a secretary crosses over more easily and naturally into administrative duties. And of course there are today many fine enterprises that have been founded and built up solely under feminine leadership. Big companies have been slow to give responsibility to women, which is quite wrong, but this is changing. There is reason to hope that soon the door to opportunity in business will swing open as wide for them as it does for men.

One final word. It is easy to become too emotional over that first big decision. Let it be clearly understood that there is no absolute best. Life is not that restricted. There are many paths to success, and what we do with the big chance when it comes to us is far more important than the initial choice itself. So I say to young people: Take it in stride. Be relaxed. Just make a start, and get on with it.

3
What Education?

*If application forms could only reveal
a man's informal education, we'd be
in a far better position to assess what
he knows. For schooling is only one part
of it, and schooling in a particular
specialty an even smaller part. The truly
creative business leader knows that his
continuing education, a lifelong thing,
is in his own hands.*

Success in business requires above all else a broadly cultivated mind.

In the day-to-day turmoil of decision making it is the unexpected that is the usual, and the responsible officer must have the widest possible versatility. He must have the courage to walk confidently along unfamiliar paths. He must not permit himself to fear, and therefore avoid, the unknown. He must be ready to undertake with zest difficult assignments which he has never faced before. The ability to adapt easily to changed conditions must be basic to his way of life. He can do this only if he is possessed of that inner assurance which springs from a mind already tested by a wide range of intellectual challenges.

He achieves this by education.

The "education" is often misunderstood, and misapplied. It should be thought of as describing a process, and not an achievement. To confuse it with graduation from a university is a basic misapprehension. The two may be related, or they may not, depending solely upon the individual. I have known business leaders who were outstanding for the depth and breadth of their education who had never gone beyond eighth grade in school, and conversely I have known college graduates upon whose minds their four years on campus had left practically no trace.

Those of us who are now in the senior years see all this clearly, but young people do not. No one can, until the lessons of mature experience bring this home to him.

Yet nothing could be more important for a freshman to know when he is filling out those multitudinous forms in September as he enters college. He most earnestly wishes to make the right choices as he selects his initial courses, and he plans roughly for the four years ahead, but he cannot possibly see the picture with the perspective that will come to him after his career has come to an end and he looks back at it from retirement.

If I might be able to stand at his side at that critical time, and talk to him about the possibility that later he might decide to throw in his lot with management in industry, here are some of the things I would say to him.

First of all, he should keep firmly before him the thought that the purpose of a college education is not merely to make it possible for him to earn a living. Far transcending this is preparation for the living of a life—a life that is useful, and filled with those deep inner satisfactions that money cannot measure, one that will release to the full, for the benefit of the society which is giving him his chance, all the talents with which he was endowed at birth.

When he thinks of business as a career, he should understand that the production of goods is not an end in itself. It is a means to an end, and that end is the happiness of the American people. Unless industrial progress serves to widen the opportunity for self development to the individual, and to make more readily attainable the living of the good life, as each person conceives that good life to be, within the framework of a free society, then it is wasted effort. A sound economy as such is nothing. It is what it makes possible that counts. This thought is often forgotten in the pursuit of private gain. But it is the ultimate reality about business, and we need to remind ourselves of it over and over again.

Finally, the young man who is planning his college

program needs to be made fully aware of the risk he
runs in adopting a specialty too soon. This is precisely
what he is apt to do if not properly counseled.

The hazard is twofold.

First, he cannot possibly know enough about himself at that time of life to choose with confidence
that area of human effort which will be most to his
taste and best suited to his natural gifts. Trial and
error is required. He needs to dip into a widely di-
vergent assortment of intellectual disciplines, many
of which he may not previously have considered at
all, in order to test and evaluate for himself the scope
of his abilities. That which seemed attractive to him
when he was in high school may turn out, when
tested, to be both dull and difficult; conversely, some
subject which had never before touched his interest
may suddenly reveal itself to be filled with excitement, and thus become his natural choice.

But even if after an honest try at other subjects he
finds himself sticking to his original choice, he would
still be unwise to make hard and fast plans too soon.
The specialty of today may be the discard of tomorrow, and job displacement in middle life can be a bitter lot.

This is the disadvantage of early specialization as
regards earning a living. It is also a limitation when
measured in terms of the living of a life. The frag-

mentation of knowledge that is going on so rapidly today erects barriers between friends and neighbors. Specialists today can advance to the point where they speak only their own patois and are unable to communicate even with other specialists, so that they are compelled to seek companionship only within their own clan. For a career to be both useful and satisfying, the individual must be able to enter readily into all phases of the life of the community and of the nation.

The answer, of course, is not to reduce specialization, but rather to superimpose it upon a general education. Like the foundation of a tall building, one's education for life should be both broad and deep. I would be the last person to deny the debt that American industry owes to the creative genius of our scientists and engineers, or to our experts in advertising, public relations, industrial relations, fiscal policy, and the rest of that galaxy of men in business who devote their lives to doing just one thing, and doing it superbly. But each business is a complete entity, and the men who direct it must see it as a whole, rather than as a series of separate compartments. This is difficult to do for a man who until middle life has never roamed outside his own cubicle.

I see no reason why a man should not devote as many years of his life to educating himself for a business career as he would if he were preparing for a profession. The surgeon, for example, takes it for granted that he will first go through four years of college, then his medical training, and after that his internship. The young man headed toward law cannot enter a law school without having first received his bachelor's degree. Why should not the metallurgist do the same thing? The fact that he did not do so in my generation may explain why, in an industry that depends as heavily upon metallurgy as steel does, it has been very rare for a metallurgist ever to become chief officer of a steel company.

Some of my friends, when they hear me express these views, say that I am merely trying to rationalize my own life. That may be true. No one among us can ever be quite sure that his ideas are free from bias. Nevertheless, I have always been glad that when I was an undergraduate I did not know I was going into the steel industry. Had I made that decision first, I am certain that fear of the competition would have led me to overspecialize. I like to say, therefore, when queried on this subject, that the educational qualifications which I brought to the steel industry were ignorance of physics, ignorance of chemistry, and ignorance of metallurgy, but a Phi Beta Kappa key awarded for excellence in English and in the Greek and Latin classics.

Those who look toward industry while in college should also understand that when they take that first job their value will lie not in what they know, but in their capacity to learn. Facts and figures should be stored in books and electronic devices, not in the human brain. Whatever factual knowledge the young man may have acquired by the time he graduates will soon be out of date, but not his ability to distinguish the relevant from the irrelevant, to analyze disparate data so as to bring clarity out of confusion, and in general to shed light where there was darkness. Particularly he must be able to depart from the specific and enter the general, thinking in the abstract, when necessary, rather than in the particular. This is very difficult for a mind trained only in technology, one which has no habit of thought other than the inductive, and no sense of reality other than that which can be tested with calipers.

To point up the importance of liberal studies, however, merely states that problem, without solving it. What do we mean by a general education?

To answer that question we must once more avoid the specific, for the formula may vary widely, depending upon the talents of the individual, and the opportunities available to him. But certain principles stand out clearly.

A liberal education is one that toughens the sinews of the mind, one that brings into play intellectual muscles not previously tested, and one that explores challenges for mental effort not previously encountered. This means that it cannot merely follow the line of least resistance by satisfying appetites for knowledge already aroused in the individual. On the contrary, it must carry him into areas of learning that are not at all to his taste, where the path to excellence is difficult indeed. This is particularly important as training for business, for he will often in later years have to undertake, and learn to do well, many things which he would prefer not to do at all.

As training for life, as distinguished from earning a living, this conscious pattern of sampling a wide variety of educational disciplines lays the foundation for continued intellectual growth in the years ahead. As a matter of fact, though not one young man in a million would think of it, this is the beginning of preparation for retirement. The broadly educated individual keeps glimpsing new vistas which, when time allows, he would like to explore further. Thus all his life he has still ahead of him an agenda of unfinished intellectual adventures. Few men read Shakespeare for the first time at fifty, but those who begin their study of the great classics at twenty never lay them aside completely. And those men who in later life search out the art treasures of Athens and Florence when they travel are usually the ones who studied the history of art while they were in college.

If no fixed catalogue of courses can be agreed upon by way of defining what is meant by a general education, what are some of the key subjects?

First of all, no liberal education would be complete without a thoroughgoing introduction to science and to scientific methods. Industry surges ahead with each new revolution in technology, and the young man who would succeed in management must keep himself abreast of each new development. It is just as important for the man whose major in college is literature to learn to be at home in an atmosphere of factual and precision thinking, as it is for the man of technical background to learn to be at home in the realm of abstract ideas. Business is a mixture of the two.

An understanding of the principles of economics is obviously significant as background education for every American citizen, but particularly so for one who aspires to enter industrial management. Without a thriving business corps, no nation can achieve a sound economy, and conversely no business can long be successful unless its operations take place within a sound economy. For the executive who makes decisions, this means familiarity with national fiscal policy and comprehension of the impact upon it of taxation, public expenditures, management of the public debt, wage determinations, and other factors that bear upon price inflation. Since fiscal policy is now also inevitably international in character, he must likewise understand the principles involved in governmental actions with regard to tariffs and import quotas, and be able to follow the implications of such statistics as the balance of payments among the nations. Without exposure in depth to the broad principles of economics, the businessman falls easy prey to the headlines of the day and leaps to many false conclusions.

One subject that is often overlooked by young men preparing for a career in management is psychology. This is unfortunate, since they will need insight into the behavior of human beings every working day of their careers. Business deals with people, and to know why they do what they do is basic to success. The answers are not all to be found in books, but guidance from a professional can be invaluable in opening the eyes of the management cadet. Alertness to the human factor is indispensable to advancement, and this should be sedulously cultivated while in college.

Proven competence in mathematics can be very useful, but it should never be thought of as more than a working tool. It trains the mind and develops habits of precision thinking, but it must not be assumed that there is a correlation between excellence in mathematics and wisdom. Business problems are not solved by formulae. Sound conclusions are arrived at only by the clear, cold light of reason, and no electronic computer will ever be developed which can take the place of good judgment.

There is another working tool which is all too seldom possessed by businessmen today, though it does not *ipso facto* connote wisdom; this is the command of a second language. Taken for granted in Europe, and especially so in the underdeveloped parts of the world, this attainment is conspicuously rare with us; this does not reflect favorably either upon our intelligence or our capacity for self-discipline. The shrinking world is not going to get unshrunk in the years that lie ahead, and we will not hold our own in world competition if we do not overcome this manifest limitation. French, German, and Spanish are presently the three major world languages besides English, and whoever can speak one of these in addition to English can get by nearly everywhere. And incidentally, whoever can master one of those languages in his mature years, will find it considerably easier to lick Urdu, or Xhosa, or Japanese, if the need arises. The time to start is in college. If a groundwork of grammar and vocabulary is laid there, proficiency can be added in later years; but without that start, fear of the unknown and self-consciousness will probably block his progress at every turn.

But the most important working tool of all which the student of management should strive to acquire is the capacity to speak and write the English language with clarity and color. Facile command of one's own language is the greatest of personal assets, inasmuch as the communication of ideas is the very essence of leadership. Wisdom and sound judgment exist in a vacuum unless decisions based upon them can be satisfactorily conveyed to others; this demands power and accuracy in the use of the spoken and the written word.

It is regrettable that debating as an extracurricular activity is engaged in by so few on our American campuses. Athletic competition can have great value for the individual, not only in the development of his physical fitness but also for its salutary lessons in self-discipline and team play; but in terms of direct application to business success, the training received by the member of the varsity debating team is much more valuable than that received by the varsity fullback.

But beyond all the various skills which may be acquired in the course of four years devoted solely to the liberal arts, and quite apart from their prospective money value as applied to a future spent in the business world, lie those deep and abiding satisfactions with which that future career can be enriched.

To understand the infinite complexity of the modern world, in which each year new nations are born which are destined to affect directly our own national interests, the thoughtful citizen needs a thorough knowledge of history. Only the past can explain the present or throw light on the future. But the past needs explanation. This is accomplished by the study of philosophy, through which is revealed to us the thinking of the great minds of all time. And most certain of all to remain with man through life, and bring him new and enduring satisfaction, is familiarity with great literature. Whether it be Chaucer or Tolstoy, Dumas or Dante, there will never be a room in his mental library, entered briefly during college by selected readings, that he will not wish to revisit in later years. Without those glimpses, however, he may never know that those treasure houses existed.

So, without detracting in the slightest from the value which a specialist can contribute to business, it seems clear to me that where there can be a choice, the particular should follow the general, and that a liberal education should be acquired first, if possible.

4
What Adjustments?

*Every successful administrator is,
among other things, a career diplomat.
And yet, if there is one besetting sin that
afflicts the gifted and promising
young manager, it is the sin of impatience:
the unreadiness to accommodate to situations
in business that he must come to understand,
and learn to live with,
before he can attempt to change.*

Once the big decision is made, and the young man not only has secured a job but has arrived in his new surroundings to make his start, he faces one of the critical periods in his life. Mistakes made then can follow him for years. Many frustrations and much disillusionment await him, and he must steel himself to take them in stride. The reality of his working day will not fulfill the rather romantic image which he has built up in his mind. He must accept this as a challenge, and, with his eye still on the future, set about making the necessary adjustments.

If he goes to the job directly from college, the contrast with the life he led on campus will be very marked.

His physical surroundings will, of course, be entirely different. If he starts in production there will be dirt, noise, and confusion, with more things to watch than he can keep his eye on, and more new sensations than he can absorb all at once. Those who are engaged in their daily tasks about him will be too busy to take much interest in him, and when they do notice him, they will be slyly enjoying his ineptitude. No one will tell him clearly what to do, and he will have to guess much of the time whether what he is doing is right.

Wherever he starts he will be among strangers. The old gang will be gone, and gone too will be the bull sessions. There will be no one to share experiences with, no one to have a few laughs with at the end of the day. If he begins in a large company, located in a large city, those with whom he works will scatter over a large area when work ends, and he will not see in the evening anyone whom he has seen during the day. This means that he must cultivate two new circles of associates at the same time, and make two sets of adjustments: one connected with his employment and one at his place of residence. His new social friends will not particularly care what his job is, and will not want to be bored by hearing about it, while those whom he sees on the job will give little thought to where he lives, or what his activities are after hours.

On campus he could choose his associates, but he cannot do that now. The choice is arbitrarily made for him by others, and here is one of the most critical adjustments that he has to make. No matter how much he may dislike that fellow working alongside of him, he absolutely must make a go of it. This is the very essence of team play in industry. He must learn to distinguish objectively between that man's good qualities and his limitations. He must build their two-way relationship on the good ones, and do all that he can to overlook those that are undesirable. At the same time, he must examine his own conduct searchingly, and ask himself what impression he himself is making on his associate. Only in this way can effective cooperation be created.

More than likely, the new recruit will not like his first supervisor. Gone will be the relationship between teacher and student. There will be little intellectual content in what transpires between them, and little encouragement for the inquiring mind. When the young man asks questions broader than the immediate task at hand, he is quite likely to be told to get back to his drawing board or desk and not to bother busy people. The professor not only welcomed questions about his subject matter, but measured his own success by the number and quality of the inquiries he stimulated. Not so this boss. He has had no pedagogical training. He may do his own work superbly, but is not usually gifted with sensitivity in

the training of young men. In fact, if he was not fortunate enough to have had a higher education himself, he may take a bit of sadistic satisfaction in making the recent graduate squirm now and then.

The recruit needs two things to carry him suc-
cessfully through these trials: first, sufficient humility
to join in the general laughter when he is guilty of a
blooper; second, sufficient insight to ferret out some
particular interest that excites the foreman, and cultivate it. This may be fishing, or baseball, or just a
certain funny paper, but the trainee must display an
interest in it too if he is to build a bridge to mutual
understanding. He must be willing to advance the
relationship upon the other man's terms, and not
doggedly insist upon his own.

This brings us directly to the core of the problem
of adjustment when a young man of high intelligence joins a business organization for the first time.
The one quality which above all others will contribute most to his success is sensitivity to human values.
He must never be withdrawn, but always responsive.
He must have acute awareness of all that is said and
done in his presence, and make it instantly clear by
his attentiveness that he intends to be a participant
in the scene about him, not just a spectator. He must
not allow preoccupation with the problem before
him come down like a curtain between himself and

those seeking to communicate with him, no matter how urgent the matter in hand may seem to him. His mental antennae must always be tuned in. The man who can only do his best work when he is alone may go far in a specialty like research, and make a very genuine contribution to a corporation, but unless he can overcome that limitation he will not be suited for broad responsibility in management.

The young man who has made an exceptionally fine scholastic record in college must also be on his guard against another weakness. The occupational disease which is all too prevalent among scholars is intellectual arrogance, a thinly veiled contempt for lesser minds. This will not do at all in business. Superior gifts must be offset by a certain degree of humility. The man with the fine mind must adjust to the intellectual common denominator about him and express himself in the idiom of those with whom he associates. He must be patient with those who are slow to comprehend, and never for a moment reveal any inner sense of superior ability.

One thing in particular which he must do is to perfect his capacity for listening. This is often hard for the articulate to do. He must learn to control the impulse to interrupt even though he sees where the comment will wind up long before the speaker has finished. And he must really pay attention, rather than just hold his breath waiting for his chance to begin. We all know the man who enters a room talking, and is still talking when he leaves. This is gross discourtesy. Team play requires an air of receptiveness from each member as he approaches others. And this must be genuine; if merely simulated, the fraud will be quickly detected.

Equally offensive is the false modesty which causes some men to refuse to express themselves when it is their clear obligation to do so. Group membership carries with it individual responsibility to make the team play effective, and this cannot be accomplished without the easy flow of intercommunicating ideas, with all members participating. There is a time to talk, and a time to keep still, and young men should early strive to acquire good judgment in discerning between the two.

When the right time comes for expressing an opinion, the young man must, of course, at all times be himself. When asked for a comment, he must give it crisply and honestly, even though he says the unexpected. No one respects a "yes" man, and the servile attempt to outguess the boss and say what it is thought he wants to hear will in the long run be recognized for the weakness that it is. This does not mean that he should start each morning off by telling the boss how badly the business is being run, but it does mean keeping himself well informed, and being ready and willing to express an intelligent viewpoint when asked.

This raises the question of the fine line that must be drawn between confidence and egotism, between belief in oneself and overassurance. Success demands self-analysis, a sober appraisal by the man himself of what he believes his talents and his limitations to be. From this must come the deep inner conviction that within the frame of reference which he establishes for himself he is competent, and fully able to meet the competition of life about him. This is self-confidence. Egotism is believing the same thing but boasting about it to others.

When doubt completely disappears, confidence is transformed into overassurance, and this is a very dangerous quality at any time of life. Nothing is more deadly in management than the assumption of responsibility by a man across whose brow the shadow of doubt never passes from one day's end to the next. If what he does turns out to be right, it will be the merest accident. No great leader, whether in business or in battle, is ever free from doubt, but he has the humility to evaluate thoughtfully the alternate possibilities and the courage to know when to close the debate and get on with the job.

This leads naturally to comment on that besetting

sin which afflicts nearly all highly educated young men who enter the business field, particularly those who choose the large corporations. That sin is impatience. They want to be made vice presidents not later than their second year, and when this does not come off they quit; this is a loss to the company and often the beginning of deep frustration for the individual. Top management in every good company is all too familiar with this phenomenon, and hard put to it to know what to do about it, for promotion in a large institution has to be an orderly affair. They do not want to kill the eagerness of mind and spirit which underlies this defect, but how to preserve it without disrupting the organization is a difficult problem.

The impatience stems in large measure from the tedium of the daily task. The recent graduate is not prepared for repetitive chores. The curriculum represented a succession of challenges—always something new. When he finished one course with better than a passing grade, he went on to the next with heightened enthusiasm. Business is not like that. When he has mastered his first assignment, the beginner cannot immediately have a new one, but may have to go on doing the same thing for a considerable length of time before the parade of promotion moves on. Waiting one's turn in a large corporation is again part of the price that must be paid for the greater ultimate security and remuneration. Young men who do not understand this, or who are not prepared to accept it, should go elsewhere. If they stay, and eventually assume senior responsibility, they may be equally annoyed by the next generation when its turn comes.

Impatience is particularly acute among those who have gone on to graduate training in a school of business administration. Having been taught the very latest techniques of management, they are appalled at what seems to be chaos that they see about them when they sit down at a business desk for the first time, and they burn to reform everything overnight. But the rule still applies. They must await their turn; when in the fullness of time their own chance to make changes comes, what they then tolerate will look just as old-fashioned to the next generation of business school graduates.

The answer to the tedium of the beginner's repetitive tasks, as well as the outlet for the creative mind which feels itself under restraint, lies in large measure in what the young man does with his time after hours. He first must choose his friends wisely. Here he is free to seek out like-minded persons and plunge himself into activities that will offer him continuingly fresh challenges. Without knowing it, he will thus be laying a foundation for self-development that will follow him into his mature years, and on into retirement. But some of these activities should be turned outward into community service. He must neither allow the sharp cutting edge of his intelligence to be dulled by disuse, or forced inward by self-gratification.

Here is where marriage becomes important. An intelligent and perceptive wife can be of infinite assistance to a man in building a career in business; conversely one who is lacking in understanding can all but wreck it.

Marriage is sharing, and the wife's first obligation is to have complete familiarity with her husband's day-to-day responsibilities, and to display an active and informed interest in them. There must be none of this "Now, John, we are not going to talk about that tonight; you must leave all that at the office." He comes home bursting—either with pride or with anger—and he sorely needs some safe haven within which he may explode. He needs that quiet, steady vote of confidence too, and the gentle prod of conscience where moral values are involved.

But it must not stop there. The wife must get her roots down in the community, and be a means through which her husband is drawn out of himself into the therapy of activity totally disassociated from his business. She must subtly put a curb on his habit of bringing home a bulging brief case and plunging into a stack of unread documents the moment dinner is finished. There must be a careful balance in the home between interest in the business and other sources of mental stimuli that will permit husband and wife to grow in stature together.

Even a man's luncheon periods should be meaningfully employed for self-development through the exchange of ideas. Just to sit with the same few cronies every noon, indulging in the same small talk, is passive. Inbreeding is as much to be avoided in business as it is in animal husbandry. Within the company, the young man should consciously cultivate as broad an acquaintanceship as he can, particularly one that crosses departmental lines. Looking to the future, he needs to become familiar with the duties of those who are in sequences of promotion that are altogether separate from his own. He needs also to form close ties with those whose responsibilities may be parallel with his own later on.

He should also establish early the custom of lunching outside as often as he can. He should rub elbows with contemporaries who are in other lines of business, and with those in other callings, such as law, medicine, and education. From them he will hear criticisms of business in general, and of his own company in particular, which will serve to keep him objective about the new way of life he has adopted. Myopia can be a disease of the mind, as well as of the eye, and this is one way of avoiding it. At the same time he will be forming acquaintanceships which will draw him into joint civic efforts such as the community fund. Thus when he finally comes to hear people identify his company as the one that he works for, instead of the other way around, he will know that he has two careers: one within the corporation, and one outside.

But to seek friendships, whether within the company or on the outside, solely because of what he hopes they may do for him, is shallow and unworthy. In the long run such efforts never pay off, for false coin is always recognized as such in the end. This is what is wrong with participating in so-called office politics. When it comes to advancement in an organization, there is no substitute for merit. It is not as simple as merely knowing the right people, for the obvious reason that the stakes are too high. The officer who authorizes a promotion for a junior puts his own career in jeopardy. He has to be right. No—the only dead sure way to secure advancement is to fill the present job to overflowing with ability, and to do it so much better than it has ever been done before that there cannot possibly be two opinions as to who is the best man for the next one up the scale. Schemers and fixers cannot stand the competition of exceptional character and brains.

There is one further and final adjustment which, though it will not affect him for many years, should be recognized early in the young man's business career. That is this: there comes a time in the life of every man when he reaches his ceiling. He has gone just as far as his talent, training, experience, and opportunity will take him, and he must accept with equanimity the unmistakable fact that his career is leveling off. This takes character and insight. Those who lack these qualities sink into a state of frustration that brings dismay to their families and their friends. Those who possess these qualities carry on with pride that they have gone that far, and find new challenge and satisfaction in the interests which they have developed outside the daily task.

Such are some of the adjustments that must be dealt with when a young man chooses business as a career. They are different from, but no more severe, than those that would be faced in other callings. They are readily solved. All that is required are self-discipline and a lively instinct for sound human relations.

5

What Is Business?

*If he were on trial for his life, what
reasonable man would engage a counsel who
understood neither the laws nor the language
of the land? If the question
seems far-fetched, ask yourself how many
businessmen you know who have read Keynes,
have read Veblen, have read Marx,
who understand the system they would
preserve and can answer its critics,
chapter and verse?*

Businessmen as a class are not outstanding as philosophers. The intensity of their efforts begets such exclusive preoccupation with the affair of the moment that they seldom pause to weigh objectively the ultimate impact upon their own lives, or upon the collective welfare of the country, of the daily activities in which they are engaged. Doing the immediate and the urgent takes precedence over the long look ahead and the final consequences. Almost to a man they are skin-sensitive to public criticism of their motives and practices, yet when the time comes when they must fight back in self-defense, they do it badly. They are inarticulate for the reason that they do not know why they do what they do, and in general they are less well informed than their opponents. They believe with belligerent conviction that what they are doing is right, and that the American system of free

71

enterprise is God-given in its benefits to mankind, but they seldom can tell you why.

Young men should avoid this mental attitude. Too much is at stake, not only for themselves, but for the future of our country. They should not embark upon a business career unless they do so thoughtfully, choosing it not only for reasons that appear to serve their self-interest, but for motives that reflect the highest obligations of citizenship. From the very outset they must strive to develop a reasoned philosophy as to why what they are undertaking is worthy, and to what extent it will serve to advance the welfare of all in our democratic society. Free enterprise is both privilege and obligation. If it fails to survive in this troubled world, it will be because we pursue the former and ignore the latter.

This system of private capitalism, based upon individual initiative and responsibility, with which we are so familiar, is under sharp attack nearly everywhere in the world today. Both its motives and its methods are viewed with bitter suspicion in many nations. This hostility is gaining such momentum, not only in communist countries but in the vast new areas that are rapidly attaining independent nationhood, that we must be on our guard. Our weakness is complacency. Those ancient traders who met each day in the Agora at Athens, as well as those who gathered around the Roman Forum, believed that their way of life was supreme, and would survive forever. Yet both were swept away. Only ruins remain to mark their place in history.

This can happen to us too. For our very survival we need dynamic convictions that are based, not upon the unthinking acceptance of traditions passed on to us by earlier generations, but upon a deep understanding of the impact of our present activities upon the world around us. We must not confuse what has been with what is. If we believe that our way of life is still the right one, let us take fresh inventory and find out why, in order that we may bring all our resources to the task of preserving it.

Once the young man has thought all this through to the best of his ability, in the light of his own limited experience, he must continue thereafter to build further his personal philosophy. And this credo, which is strictly his own, should consistently guide his day-to-day conduct in order that it may be fulfilled. Otherwise he will not be true to himself, nor worthy of his heritage. He must not merely ride the current; he must pull his weight, and always in the direction he himself has chosen.

The basic principle upon which the system of private enterprise rests is the power of the concept of personal freedom. We believe that to the maximum extent possible, within the framework of an organized society, all basic decisions which touch a man's life should be made by the man himself. We hold that human happiness cannot be imposed from without, and that the only true satisfactions are those that constitute the fulfillment of desires and aspirations arising within the individual's own mind and heart.

Applying this ideal to the material world, and to the production of goods and services, we come first to the consideration of the free market. Where a few govern the many, with full power to direct all the activities of their lives, the individual exercises no choices. He is told what he needs to make him content, and he must take what is offered. The sum total of all the decrees, when tabulated, sets the pattern of production and gives industry its target.

Not so with us. Our factories turn out what the buyer asks for. He is our dictator, and he issues the only decrees that American business recognizes. All day every day our people vote as to what the pattern of our production shall be. Their purchase tickets are the ballots. Thus we respond to the creed of our democratic way of life: In the long run the wisdom of the many is more to be trusted than the egocentric pronouncements of the fallible few.

Because the individual citizen is just as free not to buy as he is to buy, we have economic cycles. Since all of us, as consumers, are a bit volatile by nature, we tend a bit to rush from one side of the stately ship of commerce to the other, thus upsetting its balance. When everyone buys at once we have a boom, and when we all begin to suspend or postpone our buying, we have a recession. This is regrettable, but it is the price we pay for freedom.

Unhappily, not all businessmen genuinely accept the concept of the free market. There are those who insist upon it when they buy, but resist it when they sell. The sneak telephone call to the competitor by which prices are rigged is immoral, and it is for this reason that it has been made unlawful. It is honest rivalry between producers that makes possible flexibility of choice to the consumer and creates the incentive for industrial progress. Those who restrict this are placing a limitation on freedom, and whoever restricts freedom in *one* of its manifestations threatens it in *all*, and invites collectivism.

It is likewise a denial of the principle of the free market when an American manufacturer asks our government to limit the importation of competitive products from abroad by the imposition of tariffs or by the use of import quotas. Such a man ordinarily resents all interference by authority with the conduct of his business, but he is not above making an exception when it is in his own interest. He opposes gov-

ernmental subsidy, except when offered to himself.
Actually, when he is successful in establishing such
import controls, the effect is to levy a tax upon all
American citizens for his exclusive benefit by requiring them to pay more for the product in question
than would be required if they could exercise a free
choice. If we really believe in freedom as the domi-
nant principle in our democratic society, then the
consumer should have the unlimited right to buy
whatsoever he selects, from the manufacturer of his
choice, wherever situated.

Another manifestation of the concept of freedom
as related to our system of production is the accumulation of the vast sums of capital required for the
construction of our factories, the carrying of our in-
ventories, the financing of our distribution, and all
the other varied fiscal needs of business. In Russia
this is done by taxation without the consent of the
governed; with us it rests entirely upon voluntary
action. Under our system the individual, when com-
pensated for his effort, has complete freedom of
choice either to spend or to save, as he elects. If he is
prudent, he will consistently set aside a part of his
gain for future enjoyment or security; but he is not
required to do so, for freedom, with us, means freedom to be foolish as well as to be wise.

Once the individual has made his decision and

withheld a part of his earnings from present enjoyment, he has a second choice. He may either hoard those values, and keep them constantly in hand, or he may use them to add still further to his future security by investing them for gain. It is here that he becomes a part of the enterprise system, for when he offers his savings to the business community—he and tens of millions like him—a vast pool of capital is created which makes possible the forward thrust of American industry. He may do this directly, through the purchase of common stock or other securities offered by corporations, or he may delegate that responsibility to others by placing his funds with an insurance company or an institution for savings. It is his sacrifice, infinitely compounded, that is the life blood of business; yet the entire operation is at all times completely voluntary.

More and more the employee is coming to invest in the securities of the company for which he works, and this is an excellent thing, both for him and for the economy as a whole. Pride of ownership is a powerful incentive, and to be a part of the institution to which he gives his effort adds purpose to his life. Nothing could reflect greater credit on progress under the free-enterprise system than the fact that today many corporations have a larger number of stockholders than they have of employees.

Here we must pause to consider the value to our society of the single mechanism which alone makes it possible for the savings of the multitudes to be brought under unified control for the direction of production. It is a unique heritage from our Anglo-Saxon ancestors, and one that is so familiar to us that we take it for granted as readily as we do the air we breathe. Yet there are many parts of the world where it is still unknown, or at least so dimly understood that it is suspected as evil rather than recognized as an indispensable working tool for the material advancement of mankind. I mean the corporation as a legal entity. It is this concept of limited liability, the risking only of that which is put in, which makes possible the great power of production without which our life would still be primitive. I wish I knew who it was who first conceived this basic idea. His name ought to be proclaimed wherever management is studied and taught, and ought to be revered by businessmen everywhere. Unfortunately, however, he must remain the unknown benefactor.

The powerhouse which creates the high voltage that gives the system of private enterprise its dynamic drive is profit. It is here that we part company from the socialists. All who are setting out to develop their own business philosophies must understand this clearly. What holds management to its task is the desire to make a good showing for the stockholders, and this is a far more effective force operating for the benefit of society than the amiable exhortations of socialist prime ministers or the whiplash of the totalitarian dictators. Responsibility voluntarily assumed in the hope of personal advancement will inevitably outproduce that which is collectively imposed upon reluctant participants in the social drama.

It is profit that creates the required capital. The desire to earn engenders the will to save, and there is no force greater for the gathering of new funds, produced by thrift, than the payment of good dividends. Once again the power behind this important force in our society stems wholly from the fact that the entire relationship is based upon voluntary action.

Competition is the regulatory control. When the market is completely and genuinely free, the pace is fast. The producer has no alternative. If he is to make a profit, he must strive eternally to give the public a better commodity at a lower price. If he does not, someone else will. When the entire process is free all the way through, society has a built-in guarantee that each participant will at all times bring to his particular assignment his very best effort. No other system of production yet devised by man can equal this in effectiveness.

Yet there are still among us many American businessmen who do not really comprehend these basic principles which underlie the system of free enterprise, and who therefore negligently permit their conduct to cause it harm. They are honorable men in their private lives, and mean to do no wrong, but they have never stopped to analyze what goes on about them because they have known no other way.

The best thing that could happen to such men would be to suddenly find themselves set down in the midst of some remote country where private initiative and responsibility in the production of goods and services have been consciously rejected in favor of state socialism, so they could hear firsthand some of the reasons why this has come to pass.

Take Africa south of the Sahara, for example. I happen to know that area rather well, and free enterpriser though I am, I cannot fail to recognize that there are many circumstances which make the emulation of our way of life all but impossible at this time. Conversely, these elements bring home to me values in our heritage which we take too much for granted.

To begin with, the primitive African does not understand a money economy. Living strictly at a subsistence level, he and his family provide for their own wants, and what faint traces of trade exist are carried forward strictly on a barter basis. This means that he does not recognize the money incentive as an inducement for effort. If he were given a job, and if in time his pay should be raised, his instinct would be to work fewer days per week and to continue his traditional standard of living.

Neither would he instinctively understand the concept of setting aside for future security and enjoyment any part of the return from his present effort. African tribes have an extraordinary traditional social security system of their own by which they take care of their kin, and the individual would not be worried about what lay ahead, for he would know that his children and relatives would look after him. If by a miracle he did learn thrift, there would be no institutions through which his savings and those of others might be brought together in sums adequate for the financing of industrial projects. In other words, the voluntary accumulation of capital is impossible at the outset in such a society, so that there is no source of funds for the financing of industry except those which the government itself can provide through taxation and through the pledging of its credit. Finally, where this is true and where the capital is public in its origin, it is right that it should be administered by public officers, and thus state socialism is the only answer.

How fortunate we of this generation in the United States are that over the centuries our ancestors conquered those limitations and passed on to us a social climate that makes free enterprise possible!

When an American entrepreneur, equipped both with capital and initiative, proposes to enter an African country and there transplant a seedling of free enterprise, he encounters another difficulty from which again we have mercifully been spared in the United States. South of the Sahara there is no tradition for the private ownership of land, and obviously capital provided by stockholders through saving cannot be used to construct plants and buy equipment unless the management is permanently assured of its right to possession of the property involved. In Africa, since the beginning of time, land has been communally owned. The chief tells each head of a family what land he may cultivate, and makes changes in the allocations whenever he wishes. This tradition is very difficult to overcome in the new Africa, no matter how enlightened the head of the state may be, and its continuance is a great asset for the communists who are competing with us.

Finally, full comprehension of the enterprise system requires clear understanding of the contrasting social systems that prevail in other parts of the world. This the American businessman is apt to ignore. In the carrying on of our own affairs, we study the product of our competitors continuously. When someone gets a better idea than we have developed, we immediately put our research departments to work to find something to equal it or excel it, but we do not seem to do this in the realm of social ideas.

To a man we condemn communism, but where among us is a single man who has ever read Karl Marx? I happen to have done this because I went to college long enough ago to have had *Das Kapital* prescribed in a history course before it was considered subversive for a professor to do so. Today a young recruit in industry who is caught with that book in his brief case would be fired out of hand. Yet Marxism is our competition.

Actually we need to know, and be proud of the fact, that the Russians today are paying new tribute to free enterprise by abandoning gradually the Marxist principle of "from every man according to his ability, and to every man according to his need." They require increased production badly, and to achieve it they are introducing group bonuses and all sorts of other money incentives.

Similarly, go to any convention of the trade association of your choice, and you will find there that resolutions which denounce Keynesian fiscal policies are passed with roars of approval by men who have never read a line of Keynes.

None of this reflects credit upon our business leadership, and I ask the generation that is to follow mine to purge themselves of our sins.

Let us know why we believe what we do. Let free enterprise cease to be a superstition handed down to us by our forefathers, and become a living faith.

6

What Are the Rewards?

"Opportunity for ambitious young man."
So reads many a help-wanted ad, and the more
ambitious the young man, the more meanings
will he read into the word "opportunity"
as he weighs one job move against another.
For even the tangible rewards of managers
take a variety of forms, and
executive compensation means more
and different things as a man
moves up the ladder.

The young man who reaches his big decision, and chooses business as a career solely on the basis of money, will live to regret it. When at long last he comes to the end of that career he will have nothing but money to show for it, and will have missed the deep satisfactions that will have come to those of his classmates who made their decisions on the basis of how they might render the greatest service to the society that gave them their opportunity.

More of this later. The thing to emphasize at this point is the fact that such service can and should be the paramount endeavor of the businessman. Once this is accepted as a part of the man's credo, it then becomes right and proper that the place of money in his life should be thoughtfully evaluated.

The doctrine of free enterprise rests upon the principle that the laborer is worthy of his hire. We make no apology for relying upon the use of incentives to call forth effort, since the gain to society and that to the individual are in parallel. The more each man produces, the more we all benefit, and we see no reason why the diligent should be compelled to share the fruits of their efforts with the indolent.

Both socialism and communism hold the opposite view. They ignore the obvious fact that no two human beings have the same range of talents or will to achieve, and unrealistically expect all men to make the same effort, and be satisfied with the same rewards, regardless of the contributions they make. This is so contrary to human nature that some pressure was necessary, and dictatorship came into being. Now, however, it is clear that not even the whip can bring forth as much effort for the common good as the judicious use of incentives and the allocation to the individual of a share in that which he produces is proportionate to his contribution. This is the why of salary scales in business.

There is also one other factor in the use of incentives which distinguishes free enterprise from communism and socialism: with us compensation and responsibility are related, while in the other two systems they are divorced (in the pure forms). With us the man who makes the biggest decisions in a company has the largest stake in the outcome. He has to be right for his own sake, as well as for the sake of the corporation. When people read about his salary in the newspapers they are filled with envy, but they forget that free enterprise has its penalties as well as its rewards. He will not be there long if he makes too many mistakes, but if he is right everybody gains. The employees have more work, the stockholders have bigger dividends, and the public has a better product or service.

It is right, therefore, that the recruit should seek the best starting salary that he can get, provided that he does not overplay his hand, and that all the way along he should be looking discreetly for a raise.

How to get that raise is a subtle art. The emphasis must at all times be upon the performance, and not upon the asking. I have known many men who arrived at large earnings who never once asked for an increase in salary throughout their entire careers. When merit does not produce promotion, the immediate supervisor is at fault for accepting exceptional performance without due reward for a period of time that exceeds the employee's limit of tolerance. In those circumstances the employee must pick up courage and ask. He must do so only when he is prepared to take the full risk and quit if his request is denied, but having made that decision, he should make his inquiry with dignity and without apology. In other words, it is altogether right to bargain for one's services when it is clear that the period of reasonable delay to which every employer is entitled has elapsed.

Speaking with candor (though not from personal experience), I must add that there is apt to be a bit of wife trouble from time to time when the subject of salaries is under discussion in the home after dinner at night. A wife is a loyal person, and she can be easily persuaded that her husband's manifest abilities are being grossly undervalued by an employer who is brutally lacking in discrimination. She sees the necessities of the family situation with compelling clarity, but she cannot understand the circumstances of the job with equal accuracy, and occasionally someone has to talk plainly with her. It might even be the husband who would have to do this.

Both the wife and the husband must understand that the progress of business is not always upward. There are down slopes too, and people can fall down faster on that side of a hill than they can climb on the upside. In other words, free enterprise is a system of losses as well as of profits, and when a severe down cycle comes, all who had hoped to share the success must share the failures. I learned this lesson the hard way in the great depression, when in the single year of 1932 my earnings were reduced a full forty per cent, and I have never forgotten it. My employer was magnificent, however. He did not forget it either in the later years.

Salary, however, is not the only aspect of the monetary relationship: stock ownership is another, and this too needs to be thought about carefully.

By every standard, a man who sets out to make his career with a corporation should become a shareholder just as soon as his circumstances will permit. When he takes decisions that affect the welfare of those whose capital is risked in the venture, his blue chip should be on the table along with theirs. They will feel much more comfortable about his participation in decision making if he has made it clear that he is prepared to share the losses as well as the winnings. This is his answer to the current canard that a new caste of professional managers is taking over industry who no longer understand the rugged entrepreneur spirit of their ancestors.

This principle is now well understood by the better companies everywhere, and stock-purchase plans by employees have been encouraged until, as I have said, many corporations have more stockholders than employees. In fact, it is well always to inquire whether the recruiting company has such a plan. The lack of one should be a mark against them. Once the young man has signed on, it would be well for him to remember that he will be watched to see whether he asks for participation in the stock-purchase plan as soon as he becomes eligible.

Once acquired, the stock should be held indefinitely, and never traded to take advantage of the ups and downs of the market. Under modern plans it usually is offered by the corporation at a price below market, which gives from the beginning a cushion against shrinkage, but, win or lose, it must be held. In fact, I say that the man is honor bound to quit rather than give a vote of no confidence to his company by selling its securities, unless, of course, there is a desperate personal emergency.

A new element comes into the situation when a man advances to a position of such responsibility that he is offered substantial stock options. The purpose here is to keep him from leaving. The offer is a vote of high compliment, coming from the Board of Directors, which announces to all that the individual has now demonstrated such value to the corporation that a special effort must be made to keep him in his post. The spotlight goes on him, and the top management, the Board, and the major stockholders fully expect him to take up in full every such option offered. He hardly dares to refuse.

Yet he must have the courage to exercise his own judgment, and corporations must learn not to put undue pressure upon him. In fairness to his own future security, and that of his family, it is not right that he should put all his eggs in one basket. No company is that good. If throughout his working life he invests his entire savings in the stock of his company, he will come to retirement with a completely unbalanced portfolio. The officers of his own corporation who supervise the investment of the group pension funds pride themselves on diversifying widely the securities which they select, in order that the beneficiaries may be protected from unforeseeable contingencies that might affect a particular issue. The same principle should govern the investment program of the individual. He must put enough into his own company to demonstrate his good faith by sharing the risk, but not go so far as to endanger his entire future if things go badly with the enterprise. And things can unexpectedly go badly with any corporation, no matter how effective the management, if external forces operating within the national economy turn against it.

One further thought needs to be expressed on the subject of compensation: the great prizes go to those who greatly dare. "Nothing ventured, nothing gained" is still the rule. I hope very much that I am wrong, but I seem to detect a new occupational weakness in the superbly trained graduate students who are flowing into industry from our top business schools. They are specialists in management, and that is fine, for most of them have had a liberal education first, but they are so proud of their skills that they sometimes seem content to go on being specialists always. They tend to duck decision making and responsibility. Their ambition appears to be to become the management adviser to the top man, rather than to be the top man himself. It would be unfortunate indeed if the intellectual sophistication of the oncoming generation in business should chill the old-fashioned urge to get ahead. When the exceptional ones leave the school full of fire for entrepreneurship, they seem to feel that this urge can never find adequate expression within a large organization. They behave as though they believe that they would be untrue to their faith if they did not go out and found their own enterprises.

So much for the money side. Now for the other rewards in business, and these are the best ones. Let no one think that the earning of money is ignoble, but let every young man in pursuing that objective see clearly that there must be something else. If he has established no other measure of success, when he comes to the close of his career, his heart will be filled with loneliness and a sense of failure. The possession of wealth as such cannot satisfy the inner man.

First among these nonfinancial rewards is pride in

achievement. Not to ask what others think, not to seek their commendation, but merely to feel certain deep down inside that you have done an outstanding job is a satisfaction that is beyond dollar value. To be given a challenging new assignment, to conceive the idea that will make its fulfillment possible, to plan its execution and carry it through to full accomplishment, even though no other person will ever pause to evaluate it properly, is a lasting addition to one's lifetime inventory of contentment. To fail through your own weakness, even though that may never be detected, leaves a scar that will require many subsequent successes to erase. To receive a salary increase that you know is not deserved is a hollow victory. But to establish your own high standards, and to know in your heart that you have fully measured up, no matter what the world may say, is the greatest reward in life. A man may lose his money, but not such memories.

Often there is the added blue ribbon that the task when brilliantly accomplished carries with it some outward and visible sign which not even the most casual observer can miss.

Consider, for example, the man who conceives a new product, one so admirably suited to the purposes of his company that another plant has to be built, possibly even a new town—conceivably even one that will bear his name for all time. Such a man knows that he has brought new prosperity and happiness to many people, and they know it too. He knows that in terms of the consumers he has caused their needs to be met more adequately, and this will be credited to him in the press. And he knows that when the future annual reports of his company are issued its earnings will be greater because of what he did. He knows in his heart that he has made industrial history.

The same abiding consciousness of fulfillment can come to those who deal with people instead of things. Reflect upon the career of the recruitment officer in a large company. He goes to a fine university to interview members of the senior class, becomes highly attracted to a particular applicant, and sells him on accepting the offer he makes. There comes the day when the young man arrives and undertakes the duties assigned to him. The officer anxiously awaits the reactions from his colleagues to the new employee. He himself is as much on trial as the recruit. Then the young man begins to click. He is well received by those whose team he joins, and eventually he begins to be talked about as a "comer." Before long many are watching him, and quietly asking whether they may not have him transferred to their departments. Promotion starts, and steadily, step by step, the recruit rises in the sequence until at last, over the years, he is made a vice president and given senior responsibility. How heart warming that is to the officer who made that first selection! What could possibly be more rewarding to a man than thus to see his own judgment abundantly justified?

On the way up the young man himself may have many intermediate satisfactions that bear no relation whatever to his salary. Perhaps he is selected for a further period of advanced education and training in a university at company expense. Perhaps he is chosen to represent his company by offering a paper at a trade convention dealing with the particular area of his responsibility. Perhaps he is designated to appear before a Congressional committee and outline the company's position with respect to proposed legislation. He might even be sent abroad to seek out new markets, or to negotiate an interchange of patents with a foreign producer. Each such vote of confidence adds to his store of satisfactions in a manner that money alone cannot measure, and makes him more determined than ever to give his best at all times. From each such challenge, fully met, he emerges a better man, and he knows it.

Or take the realm of ideas. This might be advertising, or public relations, or fiscal policy, or collective bargaining, or almost any phase of management. Let

us assume that the company enjoys an unfavorable
image in the community, possibly because of the in-
different quality of its products, or its employee relationships, or its dividend policy, or any other phase
of its general citizenship. The young Horatius believes in his company and throws himself into the
fray, determined to help hold the bridge and resist
the onslaught of unfavorable public opinion. Articulate by nature and skilled in the use of the English
language, he begins to turn out statements that tell
the true facts, and he speaks in public wherever he
can find a suitable forum. Soon his passionate loyalty
and persuasive personality begin to have an impact,
invitations multiply, and he becomes recognized as
one of the company's most effective spokesmen.

Excellence begets excellence, and outstanding performance in any management endeavor that goes far
beyond the call of duty may bring the greatest single
satisfaction that can come to an American citizen—
an invitation to take a leave of absence from the company and devote a period of time to the public service.
Almost inevitably this will involve severe financial
sacrifice, for there are few situations where it is proper
for the employer to maintain the earnings of the individual; but nothing else matters when this call to
duty comes. The soldier offers his all to his country

in battle, and so may the corporate executive in time of peace.

This may be at the level of the municipality, the state, or the Federal Government. A man in his forties, for example, can be chosen to serve as an assistant secretary in the executive branch in Washington, to head a team that will bring economic assistance to an underdeveloped country, to lead a group that will explore trade possibilities in a particular area overseas, or to bring his special gifts to our information programs. When he later returns to his company, having turned in another outstanding performance, he will not only be a marked man among his contemporaries, but he will have acquired an intimate knowledge of world affairs and the processes of government which will equip him in later life for senior responsibility, such as being appointed to membership in the Cabinet. Above all, he will have that ultimate satisfaction which only service to one's country can bring.

A career in business, therefore, brings to a man who gives it his life not only wide opportunity for achieving financial independence, but the widest possible range of service to society.

7

What Are the Ethical Problems?

*Ethical problems exist, to be sure,
at every job level. But as a man moves up, there are
fewer and fewer "rules," conveniently made
by others, to guide and govern his conduct.
He must learn, somehow, to deal with
those questions of conscience that
he alone can resolve.*

There are young men of high conscience—and they are the only ones that I am interested in—who hesitate to enter the field of business because they have been told that if they do so they will be compelled to compromise their moral standards.

This I challenge categorically.

There will be ethical problems which they must face, but they will be no more serious than those which might beset them in any other calling. Human nature is human nature wherever found. There are rascals in every trade, but there are also men of honor, and the ratio tends to be pretty constant throughout all phases of human endeavor. I have known clergymen who had to be unfrocked, and bankers who were Sunday School teachers; professors who were removed from university faculties for moral lapses, and accountants who spent three nights a week teaching

Y.M.C.A. classes. There are doctors who split fees, lawyers who are disbarred, and statesmen who lie. Right is right, and wrong is wrong, regardless of circumstances, and misbehavior is not an occupational disease peculiar to any particular trade or profession.

The answer lies inside the human heart.

To live worthily each individual must establish in his life a code of moral values to which he adheres in every crisis. This is universal. It is not true of one career more than another. Most men base this inner strength upon religion, and as you study the lives of the great business leaders you will find almost without exception that they are men whose natures are profoundly spiritual. A man who has no moral anchors will be a menace to society no matter what career he chooses. The only difficulty with business in this respect is that the sins of its moral delinquents are often more widely advertised than those of other callings.

Business does differ from many walks of life, however, in that it is a continuous sequence of decision making. Furthermore it is often difficult to distinguish between errors of judgment and genuine evil motives. Unfortunately, when something goes wrong, the public is easily persuaded that there has been intentional wrongdoing and that what happened was planned that way.

That industry in the past has had many serious moral lapses, and that it still occasionally has them, must be squarely faced and not condoned. In fact, this is the source of most of our laws that govern and control industry. When a wrong practice develops, so that even those who deplore it feel compelled to participate, on the theory that "we simply have to do it because the other fellow does," there comes a time when a public explosion takes place, and a new restrictive law goes on the statute books.

Here are some examples.

Consider the Sherman Act, the Clayton Act, and the other antitrust laws. When I first came into industry restrictive price agreements among competitors were the order of the day. I remember being told by one officer, with bursting pride, that never in his life had he changed a price without first clearing it with all his competitors. In his code, to have done otherwise, would have been just like cheating at cards.

In steel it was the Gary dinners. Judge Gary was an able man, and by the standards of his day one of impeccable honor, yet he considered it quite proper periodically to invite the chief officer of each of the steel companies to dine with him at his home in New York, and there fix prices. I am afraid that he did not even consult them. I suspect that he told them. The stout-hearted men of that generation were doers, and not philosophers, and they did not perceive that by denying the American people the protection of the free market they were sabotaging the private enterprise system of which they were so proud. This was both economic ignorance and moral insensitivity. Hostile public reaction to such practices was inevitable, and our modern antitrust laws came into being as a consequence.

Another example is to be found in the Robinson-Patman Act, which requires that all customers similarly situated shall be dealt with on the same terms. This is nothing but elemental fairness, and good management had always followed that practice, but the unethical few created such public dissatisfaction by their conduct that punitive legislation was passed which laid a new control upon all, the good and the bad together. That this might happen was altogether foreseeable, but preoccupation with immediate self-interest overrode the calls of conscience.

Washington now has an all but countless number of agencies that regulate business, and most of these came likewise into being because of management indifference to questions of moral propriety. Consider the Federal Trade Commission, the Securities and Exchange Commission, the Federal Communications Commission, and laws such as the Pure Food and Drug Act. First came the abuse, and then the law.

Had the particular business community involved in each case paused to reflect upon the consequences of its practices and had men possessed of high awareness of moral values taken positive steps to develop voluntary codes of ethics for group guidance, the general outcry against wrongdoing would not have come to pass, and the present repressive network of governmental controls would not have been required. Unhappily, the aftermath is that the punishment does not fit the crime; it usually goes beyond it. When Congress moves in suddenly upon an ethical problem in response to inflamed public opinion, the limitations imposed are often much tougher than the situation actually warrants.

Turning to another troubled area, many of us had believed for years that a scandal was brewing with respect to corporate income tax reductions for entertainment expenses. The company-owned yacht which the president used for his own friends and justified by occasionally taking a customer aboard; the executive plane making flights to a duck-hunting resort; champagne parties in nightclubs—all these, and more, were manifestly not honest efforts at merchandising. When the public explosion came, however, the correction went beyond this and rendered it difficult to establish the deductibility of expenditures that were normal and necessary.

False advertising has been another fertile field for morale turpitude, where the product when delivered fell short of the representations made in its behalf. So has been the concealment of the true interest rate in the announced terms for installment buying. Often there the profit has been not in the merchandise, but in the misrepresentation. Other reprehensible devices have been the camouflaging of the true extent of corporate liabilities through various occult practices with respect to the leasing of real estate, and the construction of showy office buildings.

Gross dishonesty such as direct man-to-man bribing of public officials is disappearing from the national scene, I am happy to say. Undoubtedly it is still practiced in our large cities at the municipal level, especially for particular services, such as building permits, but I am not willing to believe that it is often undertaken at the state or national levels. This is an advance in both business understanding and business morality. Fifty years ago it was rather common practice for a corporation to put a particular legislator under retainer, so to speak, to represent its interests. He performed the functions that a paid lobbyist does, and neither the company nor he considered the relationship dishonest. I knew two such men at that time, one in a state legislature and one in the Congress. No reputable company would do that today; the legislators would indignantly reject such an offer. Furthermore, they would do it out of principle, and not because of the great risks that would be involved.

Bribery does continue, however, in one very crass form, and young men should be cautioned on this, for it may come to their attention while they are still in their junior years. The sordid truth is that in foreign countries some American companies who would not stoop to such things at home do go "under the table." They buy their way in, and salve their consciences by saying that they cannot help it because "that is the way things are done over there." This is dead wrong, and it must be stopped. In fact, this may be the next antibusiness explosion, and the next subject for enactment of punitive control legislation in our country. This is no way to create a favorable image for free enterprise in the remote parts of the world, and the business community should put its own house in order voluntarily, by self-discipline, before the public moves in on it once more.

There is one other form of crude dishonesty which once was widely prevalent in industry. It is one which I honestly believe is steadily being eliminated, but nevertheless I fear it is still occasionally resorted to. It has to do with the clandestine traffic in trade secrets by unprincipled employees. For example, in the old days if one company had reason to believe that the research department of a competitor had developed a revolutionary new idea that might give it a great advantage, the envious management simply bought a technician in that laboratory and received secret reports from him once a week by mail. Those who were more squeamish did the same thing by hiring away a research staff member of the competitor, giving him an impressive new title and twice the salary, but they expected him to bring his laboratory records with him.

This had its counterparts in other areas of responsibility too. A purchasing agent would receive a package of cigarettes at Christmas time, and upon opening it would find a one hundred dollar bill inside. In a steel mill, a scrap inspector might meet a strange man in a hotel room once a month, receive a roll of bills, and thereafter accept incoming cars which looked all right on top but which were very poor underneath. In bad times, a salesman might be hired away from a competitor, not because of his ability, but because of the information that he would bring with him concerning secret rebates that the other company was making to favorite customers. These bits of villainy are fading, as stronger leadership gives a higher moral tone to industry, but our record is still not completely clean.

Let young men of conscience who deplore these ethical lapses, as I do, look about them in other areas than business. The same weakness is found in the professor who takes part in a rigged television quiz program, the promoter who puts on a fixed prize-fight, or the football player who throws a game for a price. It is not business that is wrong, but human nature. The general level of morality, which cuts across all the boundaries of the trades and professions, will rise only to the extent that as individuals we all respond to ethical values.

One final moral delinquency needs to be mentioned—one that is sometimes still found in the top echelons of management. I mean hypocrisy. Public attitudes taken by business leaders in their speeches and press statements are not always borne out by their conduct within the privacy of the organization they dominate. The limited opportunity for advancement available to minority groups is an example. There are men who from the platform proclaim their devotion to the principle that all Americans must have the same fair chance, but if you were able to study their personnel records closely you would find that they have no Negro who is a supervisor. There are others who for expediency permit Negroes to occupy minor supervisory positions but do not admit them to higher levels.

Industrial relations is another similar problem area. I have known executives who have publicly declared their firm belief in collective bargaining, who nevertheless, to my personal knowledge, were doing everything in their power to obstruct the unionization of their employees. Clearly, if a man is to live worthily in industry he must not only know the right but do the right. Above all, he must always be right himself.

Let me turn now from the ethical problems that face corporate officers at the senior level, toward which it must be assumed all young men aspire when they choose business as a career, and outline some of those that may confront the recruit in his early years at work.

Ordinary cheating can be practiced in any walk of life, and business is no exception. The young man who cribbed on his final examinations will take rather readily to stuffing his expense account with fake taxicab fares and meals that were not eaten, but he would have done similar things no matter what line of employment he selected. Had he been a plumber, he would have charged for overtime not worked. The number of people who will commit such petty thievery, however, is too negligible to consider in this discussion. No man of parts wants to make money that way.

Such are not the real problems. The danger lies in the fact that because everything is new and different a man may slip into bad moral habits that are hard to break before he really senses what he is doing. His overpowering desire to get ahead may trap him into practices which serve his immediate purpose but which never really get examined objectively.

Let me give two examples.

Let us assume that he is on the order desk in the sales department of a large company, and that occasionally he takes a telephone call from an important buyer. He is very anxious to report that conversation to his boss with precise accuracy down to the last detail and to demonstrate how well he can handle such calls. Nothing would serve that purpose better than an actual record, so either he puts a stenographer on an extension or attaches a tape recorder and plays the conversation back later. The boss is impressed, but he does not know that the young man committed a basic act of dishonesty by not telling the customer that their conversation was being recorded.

Or let us assume that he has graduated from the order desk and been given an outside selling job. He goes to call on an important customer, and desperately wants to come away with a good order. He knows that he is on trial with his boss, and that this can mean a lot to him. Sitting across the desk from the purchasing agent, he notices that his man has in front of him an ominous-looking file to which he refers frequently. He would give anything to know what is in that top memorandum. Suddenly his chance comes. The buyer is called out of the room for a few minutes, and quick as a flash the salesman grabs the file, reads the memo, and puts it back in place. It told him just what he needed to know, and he gets the order. But never again will he be the same person.

When his earnings begin to show a healthy increase, he will be plagued by ethical problems in connection with his personal income tax, and he will be shocked at the wide divergence of opinions expressed by some of his colleagues on this subject. He will be disturbed at impassioned arguments in defense of practices that seem to him manifestly wrong. Here he will face a broad principle that will have frequent application in other situations: A thing is not necessarily right just because it is lawful.

When he begins to rise in the management sequence and becomes a supervisor, so that others carry out tasks which he assigns to them and work under his direction, a new and subtle temptation will come to him which he must watch for and overcome. Once more the urge to impress his own supervisors may give him an ethical myopia. He may claim the credit for ideas that were not his, and for successes that resulted from the efforts of others than himself. It is very easy to slip into this habit because it can be done merely by keeping still at a time when fairness requires that one speak out.

The important thing is to acquire an acute moral sensitivity and an awareness of ethical problems. The more I reflect upon this whole subject, the more firmly I am led to believe that the breaches of morality which are committed by businessmen are more often mistakes of the head than of the heart. They are not burglars. They do not set out knowingly and purposefully to do a wrong. They slip into bad practices because they are so preoccupied with the end they are immediately seeking to accomplish that they do not reflect upon the consequences of their conduct. This will be corrected only when right and wrong receive the same thoughtful consideration as cost and profit before a decision is made.

In terms of broad company policy, the junior will have few problems of conscience. The rules that should guide and govern his conduct are general and will also apply to many others. It is when he begins to be given responsibility that serious difficulties may arise. He may then suddenly one day be told to do something which he believes may not be right.

When that happens here are the rules, as I see them.

If the issue is not black and white, but gray (that is, if it is one on which honest-minded and reasonable men might differ), he accepts the judgment of his superiors, and carries on. He can reverse the policy later in his life when he reaches the proper echelon of management himself, if further experience confirms his belief that the action was wrong.

But if he is entirely free from doubt, if it is altogether clear to him as a matter of conscience that what he has been asked to do is morally unacceptable, he refuses—quits—and walks out the door. There can be no other alternative. No job is worth a price paid in dishonor, and no future is secure under management that will authorize or condone obvious wrongdoing.

This requires moral insight that springs from habitual consideration of ethical questions, plus high moral courage. Not all men possess these qualities, but for those who do, they bring the durable satisfactions in life.

8

What Is Leadership?

*"Take me to your leader." A line
spoken in jest, perhaps, but a telling one.
For has any group been the subject
of greater curiosity to the world than its
leaders? And what of the men who head up
its great enterprises? What qualities
do they have in common?*

One supreme characteristic of the American system of free enterprise is that its leadership is determined by processes of natural selection. The ablest man gets the job. Where unrestricted competition governs the market this has to be true, or the offending company will fall behind. Occasionally in a small organization a father still keeps his chair warm for a favored son—to the great disadvantage of the other young men whom he has hired, and often contrary to his son's real desire—but most companies cannot risk nepotism. Certainly the large companies, under constant competitive pressure as they are, have no choice but to seek out and promote only those who have the most to give to the enterprise, regardless of who they are or where they come from.

In this we are ahead of Europe. There the principle of advancement solely on merit is developing, but it

119

has not yet gone as far as it has with us. Germany, for example, still draws most of its business leaders from the old families, while in France and England it is best to come from the right school: Polytechnique for the French, and Cambridge and Oxford for the British.

Free enterprise is also clearly ahead of socialism in this respect. Whereas we allocate responsibility solely on the basis of ability that has been tested under competitive conditions, the socialists have no guide except the personal judgments of those who govern. The penalty for a wrong choice is so diluted among them that the ordinary human instinct for favoritism finds a ready outlet.

I have often wondered how industrial leaders are chosen in Russia. I strongly suspect that it is done more nearly as we do than is the case in the benevolent socialist governments which are presently found in many parts of the world. Since the Presidium holds absolute power and needs to waste no effort on courting popular favor, and since it is determined to match the United States in productive efficiency, I would guess that the Communists are pretty tough in choosing plant managers solely on the basis of proven merit and ability. Wouldn't it be a strange paradox in human affairs if the system with the greatest personal freedom and that with the least arrived at the same principles for assigning responsibility?

In every sort of society, however, and under every social system yet designed by man, leaders have emerged spontaneously when the circumstances were right and forced their way irresistibly to the top.

I can think of two, for example, who were almost exact contemporaries, and whose lives were strangely parallel, although it is not likely that either ever heard of the other. One was Napoleon, and the other was Shaka. Napoleon brought all Europe to heel; the fact that he abused his power and ended his days in exile does not detract from the incredible personal leadership which he displayed while it lasted. Shaka was a Zulu chief in Africa. Born in primitive surroundings near what is now the boundary of Mozambique and the Republic of South Africa, he whipped everybody in sight, and by sheer personal courage and superb administrative gifts brought a new nation into being. He cut the throats of his people at will, but they revered him and went to their deaths willingly, once they were convinced that it was his wish. Eventually, however, his own throat was cut at about the time that Napoleon was hustled off to Elba.

American business has had many great leaders, men who seemed born to create, to build, and to drive ahead over all obstacles until a new segment of industry had been brought into being or an older one had been transformed. Some grew up west of the tracks and were of humble origin, so that from their heritage none of their powers could have been predicted, any more than could have been foreseen in the case of Napoleon or of Shaka. Within each, however, was a precious spark which burst into flame once it was exposed to opportunity. Others were born rich, and in a way I have even more respect for such men, for I have the feeling that it takes even more character and ability to stay at the top when born there than it does to get there from the bottom when spurred on by grim necessity.

I wish that we knew more about the lives of such men so that we might analyze their motivations, examine the full range of their talents, and study their careers step by step. Almost never have they written autobiographies in their later years, usually for two reasons: first, they were not accustomed to writing; second, the great ones had too much inner humility to want to talk about themselves. Nor have others written biographies about them, except in a few cases, and then usually only in connection with company histories. I do not know why it is that the American people love to preserve through biographies the achievements of our political figures, our soldiers, and our poets, but they are quite content to let the contributions made to society by our business leaders pass quietly into oblivion as each generation comes to a close.

I have little guidance, therefore, as I now attempt the impossible—to define business leadership. I know that it cannot be done well, for it never has been done, but at least I hope to point up some of the qualities which most of the great business leaders I have known have possessed.

What is it that makes it possible for one man to strike out boldly upon a course of action which he alone has chosen and which causes others instantly to rally to that cause and support that leader with vigor and enthusiasm until the objective is attained?

First comes knowledge. The leader must know, must know that he knows, and must be able to make it abundantly clear to those about him that he knows. No business problem that requires a decision is simple. The man in charge must delve into it until he has completely mastered every phase of the problem's background, both factual and ideological, yet always keeping the broad objectives in mind. The danger here is that the executive may bog down in a welter of detail and not see the forest for the trees. Men with a penchant for mathematics or pride in their factual memories must be especially on their guard against this pitfall. Facts, as such, never settled anything. They are working tools only. It is the implications that can be drawn from facts that count, and to evaluate these requires wisdom and judgment that are unrelated to the computer approach to life.

The leader must also comprehend all the relevant ideas. He must see clearly all the pros and cons of the proposal under discussion, and must evaluate them objectively before his decision is made. Nothing so weakens his leadership and disconcerts his followers as for him to announce his plan but later be unable to explain it satisfactorily. The safeguard is to let as many as possible who know the problem offer counsel freely beforehand, so that the discussion may really be complete when it is time to move ahead.

Knowledge without imagination, however, has no more value in the direction of the affairs of a going concern than an unopened encyclopedia on its library shelf. It is just an inert mass of information. Leadership is creativity. The man out in front must dream dreams and see visions. Each fine new project has its inception in the mind of just one man, and when the great idea hits him—maybe while shaving one morning—he must be able to see the whole thing shining there in the sunlight of his imagination. From then on nothing remains to be done but to bring it down out of the clouds and reduce it to brick and mortar.

Because he has seen it so clearly, that radiance will light up his face and shine from his eyes each time he outlines the program to his associates. They will come to believe solely because he believes, and when that happens you have leadership.

Next comes decisiveness. Many men have great learning and great wisdom, but nevertheless fail in administrative leadership because they cannot make up their minds. Men who cannot say yes or no, and say it crisply when the right time comes, are not to be trusted with high administrative responsibility. They may be invaluable as counselors, but they are unsuited for the top posts. With some this is forgivable cowardice: They see the risks so clearly that they cannot bear to be held accountable. With others it is a matter of timing: They are so determined to be right that they are never prepared to admit that the preliminary discussion has been carried far enough. Actually, in any tough business problem there are usually several courses of action open, and there comes a time when the man in charge must end the debate.

It becomes more important to choose one plan and get on with the job than to go on indefinitely arguing about which is the best. Sometimes there is no opportunity to reflect at all. Frequently a very tough decision has to be made on the telephone the instant the question is raised. A man who is unwilling to do this when the circumstances demand it is no leader. For the man who dares to do this, it must be remembered that the judgment thus formed is not really a random impulse. It is rather the immediate calling into play of the man's total experience.

Next comes courage. Some men when they approach a crisis reach a state of inner panic that is very much like physical fear, and they will do almost anything to postpone making a commitment. A favorite device is to ask for one more study, or the appointment of a new committee, on the grounds that certain essential aspects of the matter have still not been fully explored. This tactic can masquerade as caution, when in reality it is just a congenital unwillingness to assume responsibility. When deferment is no longer possible on any grounds, and the reluctant executive is driven into a corner and finally late in the afternoon makes his decision, he is haunted by it all night, and when he comes down to the office next morning he may promptly reverse himself. In fact, there are men who suffer from an inclination to abandon an action immediately following their decision to do it. Such men are not leaders, as their associates soon come to know. Yet they may be both honorable and wise. The mistake lies in giving them posts as executive officers, instead of as counselors.

Courage is the conscious assumption of risk. It is

knowing precisely what the hazards are, and going ahead nevertheless, thus calling into play high intelligence and lively imagination. The man who does not know what danger lies ahead is not to be considered brave just because he moves into it. We occasionally have foolhardy men in positions of responsibility in business who plunge ahead recklessly, trusting in their luck; and if the gods of chance are with them and they pull it off, they achieve wide acclaim for their audacity. This is not courage, however. The man to admire is the one who has thoughtfully evaluated every contingency, sensed to the full the risk that he is taking, and gone steadily ahead in the face of the hazard, believing firmly that the end to be gained justifies the effort.

Now to the next point. One subtle administrative skill that marks the true leader in business lies in the use he makes of his advisers. Some men have intelligence, imagination, and courage, and yet temperamentally they are so constituted that they have to go alone up onto the mountain top of their own isolation, and there make every decision. What they determine upon may be right, because of their great gifts, but when they do make a mistake it is colossal.

It is far better to submit every important proposal to a thorough scrubbing by critical minds who know the subject well before making a decision, but doing this in proper balance requires finesse. There must be no nonsense about majority rule. The man who carries the responsibility must never surrender it. Advisers must remain advisers, and he must be prepared, when the time comes, to base his decision— either for or against the proposition—solely upon his own judgment. The real leader is the man who dares to go against the consensus.

To consult one's associates and then overrule them without giving offense, or weakening their loyalty, is but one aspect out of the many involving keen sensitivity to human relationships which leadership requires. It is not sufficient merely to be wise and strong; a man must also be instinctively a team player if he is to be given a post of substantial executive responsibility. This is not easy for some men. Overawed at times by the burdens they are asked to carry, they tend to withdraw more and more within themselves. This is a weakness. They must have eyes that are sharp and ears that are acute for the nuances of all that goes on about them. Awareness is an indispensable characteristic. The brilliant man must have patience with slower minds. The man who is proud of his heritage and of his education must have a sympathetic understanding of the motivations of the less privileged. If an associate is bringing to his work the burden of some domestic problem, the supervisor must have a sixth sense which tells him what it is, so that he may do the right thing to be helpful without having to ask questions. He must merit affection as well as respect.

Genuine inner humility is the key to such sound team play. Great leadership requires no outward symbols. Beware of the prestige seeker, the man who will be found in the center of the picture whenever the spotlight is on, the name-dropper who lards his conversation with references to the great and the near-great on a first-name basis, and the man who has the habit of recounting what "I have done" instead of what "we have done." Superior performance is sufficient. It speaks for itself in a voice that is quiet, yet so authoritative that in the long run no one will misunderstand. It needs no embellishment, no arrow pointing in its direction. Conversely, inferior performance is a crack in the plaster that cannot be concealed no matter how gaudy the paint that is spread over it.

A man may possess all these qualities, however, and still fall short as a leader if he fails to have one further ability. He may be wise, imaginative, bold, and sensitive in his human relationships, and still be ineffective if he is not articulate. Leadership demands the accurate and forceful communication of ideas. No proposal, however brilliant, has value in the world of business so long as it is locked up in the mind of the man who conceived it. It is like a diamond buried in the sands of the African coast. The man who hopes to bear responsibility with credit must be able to speak and write the English language with such clarity that those who are to support him will know precisely what is expected of them when he gives them his directions. A fog of badly chosen words can completely frustrate the best of plans, and no amount of loyalty can remove a roadblock created by misunderstanding.

Nor can any man be considered truly outstanding as a leader in business unless he can also command the attention of the public. When called upon, he must be able to interpret the purposes and objectives of his organization. Today the ties between industry and the community are so close that silence in the face of inquiry can be fatal for an enterprise, and ineptitude in reply can be very damaging. Professional public relations counseling is valuable, but it can never completely fill the gap. When the crisis comes, and a leader is under fire, the public wants to hear from the man himself, not his ghost writer.

Furthermore, for the articulate man to be effective he must speak the idiom of his listeners, whomever they may be, and not couch his ideas in words and phrases that constitute the professional patter of his own specialty. In leadership, the test of whether the communication of ideas is sufficient to motivate efforts lies in what happens within the mind of the listener. What may be clear to the speaker may be incomprehensible to those around him. Research experts, for example, are apt to be serious offenders on this score, for when alone with each other they acquire a jargon that outsiders do not comprehend. Short, crisp sentences are important too, with pauses that allow the mind of the listener to fasten on one point before attempting the next. Here lawyers are apt to give offense by their use of long dependent clauses and their parenthetical subdivisions of the thought.

Above all, the executive, in his written or spoken words, must at all times be himself. There is no place in leadership for pretense. Principle must never yield to expediency, and the man who bears responsibility must learn early that the only safe rule when he speaks at all is to say precisely what he thinks and let the chips fall where they may.

But when all is said and done, great leadership is still one of the deep mysteries of the human spirit. We all know it when we see it. We envy and respect it, but no man among us can say with assurance why some men have it and some do not.

9

What Are the Obligations?

*No, for a manager it is not enough merely
to be above reproach in the conduct
of his business affairs. He will court
society's censure and, in the end,
his own self-reproach, unless he devotes
some measure of his talents and time
to the community of which he is a part.*

Nothing is offered gratis in this very pragmatic world, not even life itself, for which many pay dearly. We must never forget the basic principle of a free society, which is this: For every privilege granted to the individual citizen there is a coextensive responsibility which should be voluntarily assumed.

This is especially true of free enterprise. Each one of us must have constantly before him the thought that what society has granted, society can take away.

This is the origin of socialism. In those nations where it has been established it represents a collective judgment that the right to pursue self-interest has been abused, and must therefore be terminated.

As I have said earlier, the same indictment, though short of socialism, is the origin of much of the network of public regulation which presently surrounds American industry. We of this generation are paying for the "public be damned" sins of our forebears in management.

Happily, today, an enlightened concept of genuine social responsibility is finding dynamic expression in our business community. Corporate citizenship is an accepted doctrine. It is now recognized that the company cannot exist as an enclave that is separated by a wall of indifference from the community around it, behind which it may complacently carry on its affairs. The company must be outgoing, and outgiving. The welfare of the business institution and that of its area are inseparable, and what touches the nation necessarily touches the corporation. We cannot let "them" do it, and swear at "them" when things go badly. "We" must be in there too. When the Board of Directors meet to consider an important new proposal, the first question must be not "What does this do for the company?" but rather "What does this do for the country?"

Young men entering business for the first time must understand all this clearly, and must make social responsibility the guiding principle of their conduct from the outset. There is absolutely no other way to preserve the system of private initiative, and private capitalism, from being overwhelmed by the rising tide of criticism now found nearly everywhere in the world. We must outdo collectivism in benefits to mankind, or the verdict of world opinion will go against us.

Individual desire and company policy must be in parallel on this. Neither can do it alone. From the very first day that a young man goes to work for the corporation, he must also go to work in the community around him, and in so doing he must have staunch support from his employer. Actually, in the good companies what he does outside will be watched as carefully as what he does on the job, and will have as much bearing on his advancement. He can win his leadership spurs outside the company much earlier than he can within the organization itself, and nothing is more important to his future than to demonstrate that he possesses that quality.

The opportunities are infinite. A good way for the newcomer to begin, if he is unmarried and living alone, is to become active in the affairs of the alumni association of his college. When he thus comes to know some of the older men in the community, he offers to help them in the civic undertakings with which they are associated. This could range all the way from teaching night classes in a settlement house to ringing doorbells as a precinct worker for the political party of his choice. If he is married and lives in a suburb, he can from the outset have a part in the activities of a church, or those of the Parent-Teacher

Association in the schools. It makes no difference
how he starts, so long as he makes it clear, both to
his employer and to his neighborhood, that he accepts continuing responsibility toward the community about him.

In my opinion, in contemporary America one of
the most hopeful indications that we can and will
preserve the concept of private enterprise is the extent
to which businessmen are now displaying a willing-
ness to solve America's social problems outside of
government. We are becoming a nation of volunteer
workers; each time a new cause comes into being and
commands wide support from willing people, a blow
is struck for free enterprise. We cannot have it any
other way. There must be no vacuum in our social
consciousness. If we ignore that responsibility, government must and will meet it, with the inevitable
result that new controls will be placed on business.
Only if we do it ourselves do we have a chance
to maintain our freedom.

Once a corporation accepts this concept of social
responsibility, what does it do about it?

First of all it systematically sets aside out of profits
whatever sums it believes to be fair and devotes them
to public projects. In its immediate area it contributes
to the support of hospitals and nursing services, and
to medical research into serious health problems such

as heart disease and cancer. It has a part in Community Fund campaigns for the maintenance of social agencies and helps the Red Cross drive. Furthermore, it does these things not only with money but with people. Its benefactions are administered by a professional staff who are as carefully chosen as those in any other department, and when big campaigns are on, it lends personnel to the committees who are in charge. Finally, it encourages its employees both to contribute financially as individuals and to participate personally in the campaigns.

One striking manifestation of the new concept of social responsibility on the part of business which has been created in my day is financial support by corporations for privately endowed institutions of higher learning. When I first came into industry, this was unheard of; today it is almost universal. At the start it was limited to technical schools from which specialists for a particular business could be obtained, but gradually this was broadened to include the liberal arts; now the emphasis is on broad service to the public, and not merely on benefit to the corporation. In fact, many companies now make gifts on the basis of selecting institutions which, in their opinion, contribute most to leadership in education, regardless of whether they have any geographical relationship to the plants of the company.

The young college graduate who becomes a part of the business community should, as an individual, share in this concept of social responsibility to education, and should do so in three ways. First, he should at once adopt a lifetime program of annual giving to his alma mater. If he will study the figures, he will find that his tuition paid only about half the cost of his education, so that he is in debt to the generosity of those who have gone before for those basic values upon which his career will rest. If he received a scholarship, his debt is still greater. Secondly, he should keep closely in touch with all that goes on at his alma mater, and never permit that line of communication for intellectual stimulus and self-development to be cut. Thirdly, over and above this relationship with his own university, he owes an obligation to the community at large to advance the cause of education for all. He should, therefore, as soon as possible voluntarily seek out a relationship with the college or university that serves the area in which he lives, and participate in its various activities, including fund raising, to the best of his ability.

When his own children come along, he will, of course, have the problems of education brought home to him in a very personal way, and as they advance through the grades, junior high school, preparatory school, and finally college he must exercise leadership in supporting each of those institutions in turn, not only for the sake of his own family but for that of the broad welfare of the community. A man is not free to criticize the schools which train his children unless he is ready, when called upon, to give his best effort to making them better.

This leads directly to the broad question of the holding of public office by businessmen. The conviction is growing in my mind that here is the Achilles' heel of our valued system of free enterprise. As a class, we are content that it should be "they" and not "we." Almost never does a man bearing substantial responsibility in industry offer himself as a candidate for Congress, for mayor of his city, or for governor of his state. There have been a few highly placed and dedicated executives who have accepted Cabinet appointments, but they have been rare. Almost never have they been willing to serve as ambassadors to foreign countries. A steady stream of criticism of policies in government pours forth from business organizations, but ask the man who makes the critical speech to go down to Washington in some key capacity to help set it right, and you will find that you are talking to an indispensable man whose business responsibilities are such that he cannot leave. We behave as though we thought that what happens to our companies is more important than what happens to the country.

This is not right. It must be changed, and the young men are the ones to change it. They should not only accept, but seek out, posts of public responsibility in the communities in which they live. In a suburb, this may be a place on the school board, or the village council, or the park district; in the city the young man may begin as a precinct worker for the party of his choice, and later advance to running for alderman. We cannot blandly accept the privileges of democracy and not pull our weight in making the system work. Fortunately, in most good companies young men are now urged to participate in such public activities. In fact, though they may not suspect it, they are watched to see whether they do. But the movement has not generally yet advanced to the point of encouraging them to enter the state legislature or Congress, possibly on leave from the company for a period of years. Yet this must come. We must not abuse those who make our laws if we refuse to have a part in their deliberations and decline to share the responsibility of governing. If democracy is to survive, no group may properly remain exempt from participation in its processes.

The holding of public office, however, is not the only area of responsibility from which businessmen are conspicuous by their absence. They are equally derelict when it comes to vigorous participation in the forming of public opinion with respect to the great issues of the day.

We seldom speak out—on anything, that is, except taxes. We are vehement, and often explosive, on the subject of government expenditures, which touches us so immediately and directly, and I am glad that we are, but as to that broad background of great issues which beset this rapidly changing world, where our actions may shape the whole future of mankind, we stand silent. In fact, I make bold to say that on most of the controversial issues with which our society is seething these days there is no group among our entire population which makes so little contribution to the development of sound public opinion as the business community.

We are afraid. We stay out of the general debate because we do not want to give offense to some of our customers, or our stockholders, or our employees. Listen in when some of us are having lunch together, and you will find that we have strong opinions on many of the great questions, but watch the papers for our comments and you will find that we are mute. Thus it happens that public opinion in this country is increasingly formed by the professionals, such as newspaper columnists and television commentators, and that in creating national policy the American people are being denied the benefit of the clear thinking and broad experience of our business leadership. This needs changing—now.

So much for the area of social responsibility that the young man must be prepared to face up to if he enters business. Let us now turn to some of the obligations that will confront him directly within the company itself.

Nothing could be more basic than the concept that he must at all times bring to his job the utmost of effort and loyalty of which he is capable. He must do not only what he is told to do, but everything else within his reach that can possibly contribute to the success of the enterprise. He must be a self-starter—not merely wait for the right button to be pushed. He must exude enthusiasm for his job and for the company, and this must come from the heart. If it is not genuine, he must quit rather than permit his life to become a fraud. In short, he must behave as though he were the sole owner of the business, subject only to the requirements of team play.

He must assume responsibility for his own self-development, and never cease to stretch the muscles of his mind by seeking out new challenges. The man in a groove soon becomes a liability rather than an asset to his company. For a business to grow, its people must grow. Senior supervision can guide and stimulate the whole process of management development, and the fine companies today place this function in the hands of highly trained staff, but it has value only for those who are eagerly receptive to the opportunities offered. Let no young man forget that self-development off the job and on the job go hand in hand.

One significant facet of character training during this process is that of learning how to accept disappointment without loss of self-confidence. Human frailty and the recurrence of error, honestly committed, are endemic in the business world, and always will be. The proper response is not anger, not chagrin, but forbearance and understanding. It may be an idea long cherished and finally timidly advanced by the recruit, which is hastily rejected without proper evaluation; or it may be a promotion, long hoped for, which is denied by the unexpected appointment of another. Patience is the essential virtue here, for in time error becomes clear to all concerned and mistakes correct themselves.

Further, when an able young man reaches the point where his merit is recognized and he begins to climb the rungs of the ladder of promotion, he owes a strong obligation to lend a helping hand to those below him who are just starting. Because of the experiences he himself has just passed through, he is the best possible adviser for those who still have those hazards to face. Often it is the little things that count most, like a friendly word of commendation or an invitation to lunch. The recent college graduate should be especially alert for those who have come from his own alma mater and should be among the first to welcome them into the organization. Then is when the helping hand is most appreciated.

The next responsibility which rests upon the newcomer to business is that of understanding as quickly as possible the purposes and objectives of the corporation with which he has become associated and the implications of its general policies. If he cannot accept them with both moral and intellectual honesty, he stops and goes no further, no matter how tough it may be to get another job, but if they are in parallel with his own business philosophy, he keeps them constantly before him to guide him. Every company has a personality, and it is part of his job to contribute to the personality of the company he has chosen. Without ever surrendering his own individuality or ever sacrificing his right to question either that which he does not understand or that which he cannot approve, once he does accept company policy, he must radiate it in all his business activities. He must make that policy come alive to all those with whom he comes in contact in the course of his daily tasks.

Right here is the heart of the private enterprise system. Based upon freedom and voluntary action, it requires the bringing together of many efforts to achieve singleness of purpose and unity of action in order to contribute to the welfare of our democratic society.

The disorder of the mob brings only chaos; order achieved by the loss of freedom defeats its own purpose. The corporate form of organization as employed in our form of society is the best answer the world has yet found to this dichotomy.

These are some of the obligations that rest upon men in industry today. Tomorrow there will be others we cannot now foresee. None are onerous. On the contrary, to fulfill them honorably is the highest sort of compensation in itself.

10

What Lies Ahead?

*Nuclear energy, international relations,
the emergence of countries that were
unpronounceable names on the map a decade ago:
these are some of the issues that have
suddenly become as much the business
of business as break-even points
and balance sheets. But what specific
problems, in addition, will confront
tomorrow's industrial leader?*

My final words are not really written for young men, but rather for myself. I cannot resist speculating as to what the problems will be that the oncoming generation in management will have to face.

By its very nature, industry is never static. Change is the essence of business. The world moves on, passing from one area of turbulence to the next, with the problems of today steadily yielding place to those of tomorrow. Obviously life has to be that way. For this reason there can never be a neat handbook, to be kept in a desk drawer, that will give the answers to business questions. Such a guide would hardly be published before it would be out of date, and success lies in bringing fresh wisdom to new situations. The important thing is not to confuse change with progress, and not to assume that just because a proposal is new it is better.

My generation is just bowing itself out, and as we depart from the management scene we leave behind us for those who are to follow a legacy of very tough unsolved problems. I am not proud of this, but I am somewhat comforted by the thought that we likewise inherited tough ones from our predecessors, and by the thought that those who are to follow us will in turn undoubtedly pass some on to the next ranks. No generation ever fully measures up and finishes its job.

All this demonstrates once more that no training for business in college can in fact adequately equip a young man for his ultimate responsibilities. Even while he is studying, new storm clouds will be gathering on the industrial horizon. All education can hope to achieve is to sharpen his perceptions, in order that he may more readily recognize and appraise new problems when they appear, and give him insight into the processes and responsibilities of decision making.

When all is said and done, no one of us would want this to be otherwise. There could be no pride in seamanship if the ocean had no storms.

First and foremost, of course, among the tortured questions which we of my generation are leaving on the desks of those who are next to sit in our chairs is the relationship between management and organized labor.

I have seen the full cycle in the growth of this stumbling block to the orderly advance of the American economy.

When I left the university and took my first job, the individual worker was almost completely at the mercy of his boss, and I must admit that some bosses at that time were evil. Most employers then, as now, were men of honor, but undeniably there were an unscrupulous few who were blind to their human responsibilities and who committed gross abuses.

Today the reverse is true. I have been privileged to know many of the top labor leaders in our country, and, while we have had our differences, I have respected them as men of integrity who are as devoted to the welfare of our country as I feel I am. But there are a guilty few who possess such power that they can bring any employer to his knees, no matter how large his company may be and how much damage to our economy may result from their actions. How to curb the abuse of power by leaders on both sides of this relationship, and still preserve the concept of a free society and individual decision making, is one of the thorniest questions of our times.

Much of the fault lies with the public itself. When a nationwide strike is on, the American people do not form discriminating judgments with respect to the merits of the controversy, and they do not bring to it the full force of aroused collective thinking to make sure that the settlement arrived at meets the demands of the general welfare. Right or wrong, they want the disturbance ended. They do not think the issues through, and they are not prepared to accept personal sacrifice in order that a solution may be found which is not only fair to the parties but which will advance the prosperity of the country as a whole.

Another responsibility which management must share with the public at large is that of the orderly and equitable distribution of available jobs among the various segments of the working population. No longer can a democratic society tolerate the existence of preferred classes who receive favored treatment. Clearly the Negro must receive in fact, as well as in theory, equal opportunity, with all decisions on hiring and promotion made strictly on the basis of merit. Women must be given equal opportunity to reach the upper levels of responsibility, a privilege which is at present almost completely denied to them. In times of slack employment, is it right that there may be two paychecks in one family, with husband and wife both working, and none in the next, with both idle? An answer must be found to dropouts from school, and fair practices established in the allocation of jobs among the very young and the elderly. What to do about mass layoffs must also be squarely faced.

When a sudden reduction in the labor force is achieved by automation—such economies greatly advance the general welfare—the workers thus displaced must not be turned loose to shift for themselves. It is such evasion of social responsibility by management that brings on the rise of the welfare state. Those who have passed the probationary period must be kept on the payroll and retrained so that they may gradually take the places of those released by the normal forces of attrition, such as death, retirement, and voluntary resignation.

These are questions that cannot be shrugged off. They must not be left to the realm of law, thus advancing statism, but must be tackled by business as matters of principle, by the voluntary assumption of social obligation.

National fiscal policy must also be faced more squarely by the industrial community. This means greater participation in the forming of sound public opinion based upon understanding in depth of the issues involved. We must, for example, resolve solidly and effectively to oppose wage demands made by organized labor that go beyond the demonstrable increases in productivity. This in the end will best serve the interest of the workingman himself, for a dollar that is steadily devalued by the process of inflation will rob him of his savings by the time he arrives at his senior years. His immediate gain, which seems such a victory at the time when the strike is won, can actually be the means of his ultimate downfall. There can be no durable prosperity for any of our citizens unless the soundness of our monetary system is faithfully maintained. It is the basis upon which our entire economy rests, and business must be both articulate and firm in defending this ground rule.

Fiscal policy, however, is broader than the issue of wage demands. It includes such serious questions as management of the public debt, the rising scale of public expenditures, deficit financing, and the balance of payments in our trade with other nations. The instinct of the preoccupied executive, when suddenly confronted with such problems, is to seek a moment of release in a blast of vituperation at those in public life who are making the decisions, and then to turn back to that urgent communication on his desk. This must change. We must accept the full challenge, and recognize that it is not only "they" but "we" who carry the responsibility.

The new force, however, which has struck American industry with explosive impact, and which had hardly touched the men of my generation, is that of world affairs. First and foremost is the crushing burden of national security required by Russian intransigence in this nuclear age. Next in line is the economic integration of Europe, which has such a direct bearing upon our trade relationships, not only with the European countries themselves but with their former colonies in Asia and Africa. Finally there is the sudden emergence of so many new nations in the underdeveloped parts of the world. Not only does each of these have a voting power in the United Nations which exactly equals our own, but they tend to seek immediate economic viability in the midst of a rather frightening atmosphere of nationalistic frenzy. This, by the way, is precisely what we did in 1776. To achieve insight into our own future we must comprehend the impact of all these forces.

Finally, the outward thrust of American private enterprise into the far reaches of our globe, seeking markets and opportunities for investment in countries which were merely unpronounceable names in a geography book to men of my generation, calls for a new industrial philosophy and revolutionary new management techniques.

It is an occupational disease with us to conceive that the world was created in our image, or, if not, that it should have been. At times we carry this so far that we seem to appoint ourselves the agents to bring the necessary transformation to pass. We expect the man in the new country to react to a given set of circumstances exactly as we ourselves would if we were in his position. We behave as though he were another American on the other side of the table, instead of a human being who has behind him centuries of cultural traditions that are completely at variance with our own.

The first obligations which rests upon an American corporation about to develop a new enterprise within a foreign country is to understand it: know its history, study its language, penetrate the mysteries of its culture, learn its customs, scrupulously comply with them, and in general qualify itself for corporate citizenship. For this the skill of the social scientist is fully as important as that of the engineer and the technician.

The second is to develop a controlled plan of corporate conduct which presents an image of partnership. This is best done by sharing the investment—through the means of a joint venture—with indigenous capital, even if that involves accepting partial financing by the government itself. It also means full opportunities for employees who are citizens of the nation in question to advance on merit to all levels of responsibility.

Finally, we must decide which contingencies we will accept as risks when we place our capital under a foreign flag, and which hazards we are entitled to ask the American people collectively to share. This problem has not yet been thought through, and it is one that most urgently requires more searching inquiry—both by management and by our government —than it has so far received.

There are many more such large questions waiting to be solved, but none are frightening; none are beyond the capacity of strong and able men.

I shall never forget that dramatic message which Henry IV of France sent to the Duc de Crillon. He said, "Go hang thyself, brave Crillon! We fought at Arques, and thou wast not there."

I invite young men to throw themselves into the fray with exhilaration and high courage. Business can be made the noblest of vocations, and I assure them there is none that can bring more enduring satisfactions if the individual fully measures up, both to his opportunities and to his responsibilities.